NOT FOR BREAD ALONE

A Business Ethos, A Management Ethic

Konosuke Matsushita

PHP INSTITUTE, INC.
Kyoto, Tokyo, Japan

This book is based on selections from four books in Japanese by Konosuke Matsushita published by PHP Institute, Inc.: *Shobai kokoroe-cho* (1973), *Keiei kokoroe-cho* (1974), *Ketsudan no keiei* (1979), and *Keiei no kotsu koko nari to kizuita kachi wa hyakumanryo* (1980).

Published by PHP Institute, Inc.
Head Office: 11 Kitanouchi-cho, Nishikujo, Minami-ku, 601 Kyoto, Japan
Tokyo Branch Office: Tokyo Konoike Bldg., 2-3-11 Kanda, Surugadai, Chiyoda-ku, 101 Tokyo, Japan
Distributed by PHP Institute, Inc., and in Asia and Oceania by PHP International (S) Pte. Ltd., 202 Bedok South Avenue 1, Singapore 1646, Republic of Singapore.

Printed in Japan by Dai Nippon Printing Co., Ltd.
Cover design by Minoru Imai

First Edition, June 1984
Second Edition, August 1984

ISBN4-569-21089-9

Not for Bread Alone

Contents

Acknowledgements

THIS volume could not have been completed without the cooperation of many people who contributed their valuable time and skillful work to its preparation. The first draft translation was done by Eisaku Onishi, former deputy director of the Overseas Operations Divisions of Matsushita Electric, who served for many years as my official interpreter, and it was edited by Erika Young. The first draft was checked and the final stages of the translation process were supervised by Tsutomu Kano, Director of the Center for Social Sciences Communication. The final editing of the book was undertaken by veteran editor Patricia Murray, presently on leave from the Center for Social Sciences Communication, who did a most admirable job of polishing the translation into a smooth, readable style. I am deeply grateful to these four people, and to Kiyoko Kizaki, Lynne E. Riggs, and Manabu Takechi, also on the staff of the CSSC, for their dedicated efforts in producing this book. I would also like to thank Katsuhiko Eguchi, with whom I have worked closely for many years, for writing the introduction.

Preface

Eighty years have passed since I left my hometown and became an apprentice at the age of nine. Throughout these years my life has centered around business. I have watched the world change profoundly and rapidly, and through it all, have accumulated a great deal of experience in the field of business. My experiences have convinced me that no matter how confusing or chaotic the world may become, one can always improve his management techniques and make his business prosper. The present age is called a time of "upheaval" or of "transition," and very complex problems continue to plague business and management, but I believe there are an unlimited number of ways for coping with those problems. In order to identify the right method and know the proper timing for dealing with particular problems, a person must gain a firm grasp of the essentials of business and the secrets of successful management, and he must devote himself wholeheartedly to his work. If he is truly sincere and conscientious, he will survive recession or any other difficulty that may come his way, and make trying times into the building blocks for new growth.

It goes without saying that the management of business is

complex; there is always more to learn, no matter how many years one works in it. Yet in a way, management is also quite simple. If you grant that a business exists because it is necessary to society—because it responds to people's needs—the basic rule of management is self-evident: learn what the people want and respond accordingly. Of course, one must be conscientious in his efforts to serve the people and do his best to satisfy them. I have made this my basic principle since I founded Matsushita Electric more than sixty years ago.

A few years ago I published *Thoughts on Man*, an English translation of one of my early books presenting my views on the nature of man. This work was favorably received and its readers indicated their interest in hearing more about the ideas on business and management I have conceived over the years. *Not for Bread Alone: A Business Ethos, A Management Ethic,* which came into being in response to this interest, recounts approaches to business and methods of management that I have developed out of my own experience.

More than seventy articles selected from four of my earlier books published in Japanese on business and management have been translated and edited for this volume. It is divided into two parts. Part One is subdivided under seven themes, all dealing with what I believe to be the right approach to management and the ideal manager. It contains 53 articles on such topics as how to train and make the best use of personnel, a company's most valuable resource; how those in industry can experience the joy of creation, and how the spirit of "coexistence and co-prosperity" between the corporation and society should be reflected in day-to-day business operations. These articles are drawn from three books, *Shobai kokoroe-cho* (A Businessman's Book of Precepts) [1973],

Keiei kokoroe-cho (A Manager's Book of Precepts) [1974], and *Keiei no kotsu koko nari to kizuita kachi wa hyakumanryo* (The Million-Dollar Knack of Management) [1980].

Part Two consists of eighteen articles from *Ketsudan no keiei* (Decisions in Management) [1979], arranged in chronological order, in which I look back on various management decisions I have made and how I dealt with various crises or difficult problems, giving concrete examples from my experience. Those involved in management are aware of the pressure on them in day-to-day matters to come up with the right decisions, no matter what is at stake. I have added this section in the hope that it may prove useful to those faced with the difficulty of making appropriate decisions.

There is much more about business and management that I would like to say than I have been able to include in the limited space permitted by this volume, but rather than attempt to present all my ideas comprehensively, I have sought to share those thoughts and experiences that are basic to the conduct of business and management and recount the concrete methods I have adopted during my career.

There is no one answer in management; if there are one hundred businessmen, there are also one hundred ways to do business. Outside of Japan, too, where most of the readers of this book will be, customs and manners are quite different from ours, and the techniques or methods described here may be of little use in a different social context. However, if my readers, many of whom may have encountered Japanese businessmen in their own countries, can gain through this book a better grasp of the thinking of people in business and management in this country, I shall be gratified.

I am now eighty-nine years old. I lost my parents and older brothers while I was still young and have suffered from a chronic lung condition. My condition often forced me to rest in bed for extended periods, and even in the early days I often had to direct my staff and associates from bed. Yet I have survived, and I am profoundly grateful that I have been granted so many years to engage in work I have enjoyed so immensely. Though I may be aging physically, I feel as young at heart as any of my juniors. I continue my efforts to cultivate in myself the "way of management." In closing, let me share with you a verse, in translation, which has been a favorite of mine for more than ten years.

> Youth is youngness at heart.
> Youth is eternal for those
> Who are full of faith and hope
> And greet the challenges of each new day
> With courage and confidence.

KONOSUKE MATSUSHITA

May 1984

Introduction

Konosuke Matsushita was born November 27, 1894, the third son and youngest of eight children of Masakusu, a rice farmer, and his wife Tokue, in the countryside of Wakayama prefecture, an agricultural region southeast of Osaka. His father was a member of the local assembly and was employed for a time in the village government offices. The Matsushita family held lands passed down for generations and was quite well off, and Konosuke's early childhood was happy and carefree. But in 1899, the family went through a profound crisis. The Sino-Japanese War of 1894–95 was followed by a period of economic growth, and stock and commodities exchanges were set up throughout the country as a means of stimulating local industry. Many people were caught up in the rush of speculation, and Konosuke's father was one of them. Not long after he began investing in the local exchange, catastrophe came; the market crashed, and Masakusu lost his entire holdings, including the ancestral home and lands.

Following upon that disaster, both of Konosuke's two older brothers died, and Masakusu, unable to lead his family out of destitution himself, pinned his hopes on Konosuke, who became the Matsushita heir at the age of four. At nine, Konosuke left primary school and went alone to live in Osaka, where he became an apprentice in a charcoal brazier shop. In 1905 he moved to a bicycle wholesale house and succeeded in completing a six-year apprenticeship. In those days, the lot of the apprentice was far from easy; many times throughout the six years, Konosuke thought of leaving, but, sustained by his father's dream of restoring the family fortunes, he stayed with the bicycle shop. In 1906, before that dream could be realized, Masakusu died after an extended illness.

In the years following Japan's victory in the Russo-Japanese War in 1905, Konosuke was witness to a dramatic transformation going on in the city of Osaka. Electric streetlights began to replace the gas and oil streetlamps, Western-style buildings arose one after another along the streets, and electric streetcars packed with people clanked along the main thoroughfares. Watching the streetcars, the young Matsushita found himself fascinated by the world of electricity. He made up his mind at that point to devote his career to the promising new electric industry.

His venture into this new field began in 1910, when, at the age of fifteen, he joined the Osaka Electric Light Company as a trainee wiring worker. He worked even harder than he had as an apprentice and rose quickly, reaching the coveted position of inspector in a short five years. But while his new status gave greater responsibility, it required much less actual work than the technical jobs he had been doing. Konosuke, a bright, hard-working young man of twenty-two, fully aware of the tremendous potential in electric power, quickly grew restless and frustrated with the dull routine of his new position. He was, however, troubled by ill health, which forced him to rest for extended periods at home. His desire for more challenging work that he could engage in at home gave him the idea of starting a business of his own.

He had been working on a new design for a socket for some time, and when his suggestion that his invention be mass-produced was rejected by the company, he decided to resign and go into business for himself. It was 1917 and Matsushita was still twenty-two. Right after he left Osaka Electric, he began making plans to manufacture his socket, investing all his savings, as well as all the money from his severance pay. Even then, he lacked sufficient funds, and production of the socket did not go as smoothly as he had expected. Finally, with the help of a loan from a friend, and money his wife obtained by pawning her kimonos, and with an unexpected order for electric fan insulating plates that came in at the end of the year, his venture turned its first profit. The following year, on March 7, 1918, the Matsushita Electric Appliance Factory was officially launched, with himself as proprietor and his wife Mumeno, and brother-in-law, Toshio Iue, then just fifteen (he later founded Sanyo Electric Company), as employees.

Matsushita continued to produce the insulating plates for electric fans, and also began work on an adaptor plug for household use. In the early days of electricity, households were typically equipped with only a single electric outlet placed in the ceiling of the main room. Matsushita accurately foresaw the demand for his design, which allowed each household to use two electric appliances simultaneously. Then, when his next project—a shell-type battery bicycle lamp—was completed, and began to sell rapidly throughout the country, the company was well and truly on its way to success.

His inventiveness was matched by his flair for entrepreneurship. In the bleak years following World War I, for example, when credit was tight and most companies were retrenching, Konosuke Matsushita decided to build a new factory. This bold step served to motivate and inspire his employees, resulting in unexpected growth in production. This was a case of what Matsushita calls "positive management," but he was especially innovative in his management strategy.

In 1925, he registered the brand name "National," and two years later put on the market his first product under that brand, a square, battery-powered flashlight. Confident of its utility, Matsushita used an original marketing technique whereby he first distributed 10,000 free sample units to retail stores. This novel approach not only succeeded, but established the National reputation for quality. (Today Matsushita Electric products are also known by the names Panasonic, Technics and Quasar.)

Konosuke Matsushita later recounted how he hit upon the name National, as follows:

> I was looking for a suitable name for the flashlight, and I had about ten or twenty possibilities, but none really seemed right. Then one day, I happened to spot the word "international" in the newspaper. Somehow it struck the right chord. I didn't know any English, however, and at first I thought perhaps it was connected with the Russian Revolution or something. Looking it up and finding out what it meant, I also learned the word "national," meaning "of or relating to a nation or people." There, I thought, I've got it; the meaning is right, in fact and in name. It represents something of the people.

In those days, large, well-established companies considered brand names other than their own unnecessary in selling their products. Matsushita was ahead of his times. He was convinced that he had an economical and convenient product in his flashlight, and he was confident that it would become a household necessity. That conviction led him to go ahead and put it into mass production and strive to make it a popular manufactured item, even during a recession. His efforts paid off and demand grew quickly enough that the price was reduced several times; in no time the National flashlight had indeed become a household item. Matsushita says that he learned the trick of broadening demand through mass production and reducing the price from reading the biography of the American pioneer in automobile production, Henry Ford. He wrote,

> Henry Ford's approach was aggressive and creative, but it was also geared to the needs of society. Of course he wanted to profit by his enterprise, but he realized that the real profits, for himself and others, would depend on how thoroughly his product became a part of the lives of ordinary people, and how well it served the national livelihood. That is why he was able to continue reducing the price of his automobile, allowing more and more people to own one, and gradually expand his enterprise... He provided the means for the rapid development and popularization of the automobile.

Matsushita Electric's enterprise expanded to include wiring fixtures, bicycle lamps, electric heating devices, radios, dry-cell batteries, and many others. Each new product soon began to reach the mass market, reaffirming Matsushita's view that responsibility to society was the core of sound business procedures. On May 5, 1932 he called all his employees together and spoke to them about his philosophy of business:

> The mission of a manufacturer is to overcome poverty, to relieve society as a whole from the misery of poverty and bring it wealth. Business and production are not meant simply to enrich the shops or the factories of the enterprise concerned, but all of society. And society needs the dynamism and vitality of business and industry to generate its wealth. Only under such conditions will businesses and factories truly prosper.... The real mission of Matsushita Electric is to produce an inexhaustible supply of goods, thus creating peace and prosperity throughout the land.

Matsushita did not stop at simply announcing his mission; he declared the next two and a half centuries to be the period during which that mission was to be accomplished, and divided that 250 years into ten, twenty-five-year phases. He called the first ten years of each phase the period of construction, the second decade a period of application, and the final five years a period of "fulfillment." He reminded his listeners that day that this first twenty-five year phase coincided with their own careers.

He also announced that May 5, 1932 would thereafter be celebrated as the most memorable day for Matsushita Electric, since it represented the beginning of its corporate mission in society. Thus, even though the company was actually founded on March 7, 1918, each year it celebrates the anniversary of its founding on May 5. As of May 5, 1984, the company is in the third phase of its advance toward fulfillment of the collective mission.

Since 1932, the company has achieved remarkable maturity. Konosuke Matsushita has sought to strengthen the sense of mission among his staff and make that attitude a creative, permanent element in the company ethos. Believing that strong leadership is needed on a day-to-day basis, and in order to provide principles to guide daily activities and to encourage everyone in the company, he set forth the following code in July 1933:

1. spirit of service through industry
2. spirit of fairness
3. spirit of harmony and cooperation
4. spirit of striving for progress
5. spirit of courtesy and humility
   (later, in August 1937 he added two more points:)
6. spirit of accord with natural laws
7. spirit of gratitude

These seven principles remain today, as they have been since that time, the basic watchwords for the daily work of tens of thousands of Matsushita Electric employees.

Konosuke Matsushita's thought as a businessman developed in the form of new and concrete principles and approaches. In 1933, he divided the company into three divisions, giving each autonomous decision-making power. Division One was responsible for radios; Division Two for lights and batteries, and Division Three for wiring implements, synthetic resins, and electric heating appliances. The division heads were put in charge of the management of each respective sector—in what Matsushita called "autonomous management"—and this provided the framework in which the Matsushita Electric tradition of management has been fostered and passed on to younger generations of managers.

World War II plunged Japan into a period of confusion and chaos, confronting Matsushita Electric with the most difficult dilemmas since its founding. The day after Japan's surrender,

Konosuke Matsushita gathered his executive staff together, and announced his plans for the reconstruction of the company. Production, he declared, would provide the base for national rehabilitation, and now they must devote themselves in earnest to the rebuilding of their country. He called on all the employees to commit themselves to a new beginning and mobilize their resources to meet the task before them.

The General Headquarters of the Allied Occupation, however, began to enforce its policy of dismantling the huge industrial concerns, the zaibatsu which had dominated the Japanese economy since the prewar period. Along with the rest of Japan's large companies, Matsushita Electric was included at first among the targets of this policy (since it was not a zaibatsu, it was later exempted). All the directors of the company under Matsushita were purged, company assets were temporarily frozen, and all manner of problems arose, but with the united efforts of all employees, the company managed to overcome its setbacks and rebuild itself. In the more than twenty years that followed, it matured into a corporate group with one of the largest gross sales figures in Japan, and was ranked 39th among the world's largest industrial corporations listed by *Fortune* magazine in its August 1983 issue.

As he strove to rebuild his business from the destruction wrought by the war, Konosuke Matsushita looked around him at the chaos into which Japanese society had fallen. He began to study how mankind could free itself from pain and suffering and attain happiness, and build a peaceful, harmonious society. On November 3, 1946, he founded the PHP Institute, the initials standing for "peace and happiness through prosperity." Its goal is to achieve a peaceful society richly endowed both materially and spiritually. In 1980, the Matsushita School of Government and Management was opened, dedicated to the search for ideas and policies in education, economics, politics, and other fields that will contribute to progress and development in Japan and the world in the twenty-first century. Its main goals are to train and nurture potential leaders for the future capable of resolving the many problems facing Japan.

Three years later, in May 1983, Matsushita launched a unique new project called the Kyoto Colloquium on Global Change. It is designed to consider the ideal patterns of society and life in the world and Japan in the twenty-first century and beyond and to formulate proposals for ways to work toward that goal. This study group plans to share the results of its research with the people of Japan and all other countries, presenting concrete proposals to world leaders in an effort to help set the direction for human society in the current period of transition.

KATSUHIKO EGUCHI
Managing Director
PHP Institute, Inc.

PART ONE

Chapter One
Human Resources

1. An Objective Sense of Self

WHEN you think about it, a private enterprise is really a public institution, insofar as it is expected to contribute some benefit to society as a whole. Given the public nature of its raison d'être, a private firm, large or small, must help its members grow as people and become responsible citizens. The young men and women who join a company that has a personnel policy designed to enrich their human potential are fortunate indeed.

A sense of self and the ability to be objective are qualities that I believe corporate management should try to cultivate in employees. Sound sense and good judgment are important for anyone, but especially for businessmen. A businessman must face all kinds of situations that can change from one moment to the next. He must perceive the situation accurately and respond—often quickly—with the most appropriate decision. One cannot assess a situation correctly, however, unless he knows his own strengths and weaknesses. A company, or any group for that matter, composed of people who know themselves and who can deal adequately with any given situation will be successful. That kind of group, furthermore, will work together well, free of internal schisms.

An organization whose members lack perspective and an objective sense of self, on the other hand, will probably not last very long. Its individual members may be competent and have all the right information, but they will not be able to pass sound, unified judgment on the problems that confront them.

Still, we are all human; only God can know the truth about everything. We have no way of knowing what is absolutely correct or of judging the truth. It is impossible to teach your employees how to assess a situation correctly. But you can tell them always to remember the importance of sound judgment, and they can learn by experience. The person with a sense of self is aware of his own imperfections and, at the same time he is determined to be accurate in his evaluation of a situation. Without those qualities, including the willingness to keep trying, he will not go far in business.

Managers and workers alike must never cease the effort to develop the ability to make sound judgments. A company composed of such individuals will be strong and prosperous, and will be able to multiply its contribution to society.

2. Trust Your Employees

PEOPLE often compliment me on the way I handle personnel management. "What is your secret?" they ask. That is hard to answer, since I do not have any special conscious techniques. All I can do is explain my basic attitude toward the people who work for me.

There are several ways of managing one's employees. One, apparently, is to use extraordinary wisdom and exert charismatic leadership in order to inspire workers to do their best. I have never approached my job that way since, lacking both those qualities, I do not belong to this category of manager. I am the type who consults his staff and asks for *their* wisdom. I have found that people are generally more willing to cooperate when you solicit their advice than when you try to tell them how to do everything. If I have any "secret," it is a natural inclination to trust my staff and seek their cooperation.

I do not claim that my approach is always workable or

widely applicable. An exceptionally competent manager who is capable of arriving at the right decisions without consulting his subordinates will get the job done the most efficiently by issuing orders. Such streamlined management often brings great benefits to the company and everyone concerned.

If a manager does not have that sort of capability, then my style of personnel management is perhaps more desirable. I often have the feeling that any one of my employees is more competent and more knowledgeable than I am. Perhaps because I had very little formal education, I am prone to admire others for their achievements and skills. I trust my employees for what they know and what they have. So when I want to get something done, I tell one of them, "I can't do it but I know you can." Someone who knows he is trusted tries to do his best and eventually succeeds.

All this should not be taken to mean that I never give orders and never scold my employees. In my capacity as president or board chairman, I have had to use strong words on occasion in reprimanding people on my staff for their failures or blunders. But I have never thought myself superior to them in intelligence or knowledge.

An observation I have made over the years is that companies whose top management trusts and praises their employees are by and large successful. In contrast, when the president is the type who complains frequently about staff incompetence, the company itself is usually in trouble. I have no statistics to prove this, but I believe there is some truth to it. The "I am better than you" attitude on the part of the top person can cost him his entire business. A genuine sense of humility, on the other hand, will give him huge dividends, both tangible and intangible.

3. A Priceless Opportunity

ONCE a junior executive in my company made an error serious enough that I could not overlook it. I wrote him a letter containing an official reprimand, but before giving him the letter, I called him into my office to tell him what I was about to do. I then asked him how he would react to getting a letter from me regarding his misconduct. "If you don't think you deserve it, then there is no point in giving it to you," I told him. "But if you acknowledge your wrongdoing and are sorry for it, then it is worth the trouble, as it might help you improve your performance in the future. If you think the letter of reprimand is too late to change anything and, therefore, useless, I won't give it to you."

The young man said he would be happy to receive the letter. Just as I was about to hand it over, his immediate supervisor and one of his colleagues walked into the room.

"You have come at an opportune moment," I said to them. "I was just about to give your associate a letter of reprimand, which he says he is happy to receive. I am very pleased at his attitude." I told them that I would like to read the letter to them so they could be witnesses to it.

After reading the letter, I told them that I thought they were all lucky to have someone to tell them off. "If I made such a mistake," I said, "there is no one who would say anything right to me, but you can bet there would be a lot of criticism behind my back. And it doesn't help at all. I would go on making the same error. It is good that you have me and others to point out your mistakes and tell you to shape up. Once you are promoted to top positions, no one is going to protest, no matter what you do. That is why you should consider this a priceless opportunity."

My approach in this case was probably not altogether orthodox, to say the least, and I know it would not necessarily work in another situation. But the person in question took me seriously, and later he became an outstanding manager.

4. Everyone Is an Asset

HIGH caliber skills in executing a job and working with others are in great demand today, but they are hard to find in the same person. In every corporation, top management is constantly trying to raise the quality of their personnel through recruitment and training programs, but it takes a great deal of perseverance as well as wisdom and resourcefulness on the part of the manager to improve the caliber of his staff.

How do we go about educating our employees, and what can managers do to help each worker grow? There are as many answers to these age-old questions as there are managers, but for me, one method seems to have worked over the years quite well. Basically, that is to deliberately seek out the positive qualities in each person, and never try to find fault with him. This has been easy for me, partly because of my own propensity to notice the merits in people before I see their demerits, and partly because I have more peace of mind if I approach people that way.

If I tended to see only the negative side of an employee, I could never assign him to a responsible job without feeling qualms. I would be constantly worried about him making some very damaging error. To be so preoccupied would affect my performance as manager; I would not be able to concentrate on the more important policy matters of the company.

What is worse is when a manager's lack of trust and confidence in the workers inhibits him from any bold moves or radical measures. If he does not dare to act boldly when circumstances demand it, his company as a whole is going to suffer.

All said and done, however, I must confess that at times I overestimate people, putting them into positions they are not ready for. But I would rather overrate the abilities of my employees than underestimate them. It often turns out that if you put a person in a post and give him your full confidence, he does his best to live up to your expectations. Whether the person is appointed department manager or director of a subsidiary, he usually "grows into the job," gaining abilities commensurate with his new responsibility.

A person makes a position; if he is incompetent, his position will suffer, and if he is competent, the prestige and authority of his position will grow. Despite all the talk about the "level of incompetence," I believe that most people are perfectly capable of learning to do the job they are assigned to, and doing it well.

But they must work harder than ever before. Their supervisor must constantly encourage them, helping them to overcome their shortcomings and weaknesses. I would say that a manager ought to give at least seventy percent of his attention to the positive qualities of his subordinates; thirty percent is enough for those points that need improvement or changing. Employees, for their part, should try to see the strong points in their managers as much as possible. Positive attitudes on both sides will augment the productivity of the team, and contribute to the personal growth of all concerned.

5. For Bread *and* Values

I know the analogy probably sounds outrageous, but I wonder if there is not a certain parallel between childrearing and employee education. I am talking about the crucial importance in both of conviction. If we want to bring up our children properly, we need to have clear ideas of the basic goals in a life of integrity and humanity, and how to be a good member of the family and community. Everyone has a different world view and outlook on life; one is not necessarily right and the others wrong. The important thing, whatever our outlook, is never to vacillate in our attitudes toward the basic issues. When parents have firm convictions, they will be consistent in what they say and do and in the way they treat their children. That approach will have only a positive influence, and will be of great help in guiding them in the right direction as they grow up.

People in top management also need firm, well-formed views on society, business, and life if they are to exert a solid influence on those under their supervision. When senior executives are consistent in their thinking and behavior, their subordinates will trust them and follow their examples with a sense of security. But corporate management requires a little more than conviction and consistent attitudes. It needs what I call a sense of purpose.

Every company, no matter how small, ought to have clear-cut goals apart from the pursuit of profit, purposes that justify its existence among us. To me, such goals are an avocation, a secular mission to the world. If the chief executive officer has this sense of mission, he can tell his employees what it is that the company seeks to accomplish, and explain its raison d'être and ideals. And if his employees understand that they are not working for bread alone, they will be motivated to work harder together toward the realization of their common goals. In the process, they will learn a great deal more than if their objectives were limited to pay scales. They will begin to grow as people, as citizens, and as businessmen.

One can gain the required knowledge and experience over the years simply working with a company, even if its management has no sense of mission to share with the employees. But knowledge and experience alone will not help one develop into a person of wisdom, with maturity and depth to his personality. What he needs is a philosophy that gives a frame to his thoughts and guides his behavior. Top management can assist in the employee's personal growth by spelling out the company's philosophy.

6. On-the-Job Experience

EACH spring, young people fresh out of college join our company; they all undergo a period of orientation and training at factories or sales outlets. When the company was still small, there was no need for this kind of program, because on-the-job training alone was enough to give the employee an overall perspective of our operations. Even white-collar workers were closely involved in day-to-day production and sales activities. Engineers responsible for research and development and those engaged in design work actually tightened screws and assembled parts on the shop floor in the course of their daily routine. Men in charge of marketing and sales planning were in direct contact with the dealers. They were aware of exactly what was going on in the front line of the market.

As the company grew larger, however, work became more

specialized and more compartmentalized. On-the-job training in the area of one's specialty is still useful and necessary, but it can no longer prepare the employee adequately for a long career with the firm. That is why we try to send all our new employees to factories and sales outlets for broad, practical experience before assigning them to a particular slot in the corporate apparatus.

In a way, a businessman is like a practicing physician; he must have broad "clinical" knowledge and experience, in addition to theoretical knowledge in his special field. No matter how conversant with medical theory, a doctor cannot treat a patient with confidence or conscience unless he also has a certain amount of clinical practice behind him. Likewise, a business school graduate cannot be called a businessman until he gains some practical experience.

Suppose a man who never actually has been a salesman becomes a sales manager. He sits down at his desk and tries to draw up a marketing plan. He may be bright and competent, but his plan will be based on ideas and second-hand knowledge. Chances are that it will be of little practical use and will ultimately fail. If, on the other hand, the sales manager has undergone two or three years of apprenticeship at a retail store or a wholesale company and has mastered the basics of sales that way, any plan he conceives later will reflect his first-hand knowledge of the business.

Similarly, college-educated engineers with no production-line experience would have difficulty designing or developing a good product with a high degree of manufacturing feasibility. A few years of workshop experience at a young age gives them a clear notion of how their designs and ideas are incorporated into the finished products. That knowledge can only have a positive influence on their research and development work.

A period of apprenticeship for young college-educated workers is just one of many approaches to personnel training. What is most important to remember is that businessmen and engineers are more like clinical practitioners than academicians or theoreticians.

Chapter Two
Collective Wisdom

1. Tail Trails the Head

EMPLOYEE training is the fad of the day. Corporations large and small, even retail stores, all seem bent on educating their workers. They hold special in-house study sessions and training programs, and send their employees to seminars and classes organized by outside agencies. All large companies have independent facilities for employee training, invariably furnished with the most up-to-date audio-visual equipment.

There is nothing wrong with management enthusiasm for developing the potential of its employees; it is highly commendable. After all, it is the caliber of your work force that makes the difference in your business. Well-thought-out programs and well-equipped training centers are certainly worth the time and money. But we must also remember that programs and facilities provide no more than an institutional framework. They are impersonal, neutral "things" that cannot feel, sympathize, or reason. If, as it appears, the framework is here to stay for a while, someone must humanize it—but who? And how?

In a shop, I believe it is the proprietor who must inject the human quality into personnel education. In the case of a company, it should be the president. Through his or her dedication to work and unfailing loyalty to the firm, the top person must set the example. Of course no one is perfect, and no proprietor or manager can be expected to be impeccable in everything he does. That is asking too much of an ordinary businessman. And, in fact, who would want to work for a paragon of perfection? With such a presence always hovering over the firm, you could never relax. Every manager, if he is human, has his shortcomings. His very fallibility gives him valuable common ground with those working for him. They know he will make mistakes, too, but the one area where he cannot fail, where he must be exemplary, is his commitment to his work.

No matter how knowledgeable or talented a manger is, he will not make a good leader if he appears to be even slightly ambivalent toward his work. His subordinates will be able to look to him for a model worker or a committed leader. As an old saying goes, "The tail trails the head." If the head moves fast, the tail will keep up the same pace. If the head is sluggish, the tail will droop. From a hard-working proprietor, employees can learn the virtue of diligence. In this case, as in others, the direct object lesson is far more effective than any formal training program.

The proprietor or manager must also be willing to listen to what his subordinates have to say about management and day-to-day operations. That attitude is a necessary part of successful management based on the collective wisdom of the firm, and it is also important in motivating employees and helping them grow. If top management has no ear for the opinions of its workers, bottom-up communication will soon dry up, leaving a dangerous void. Workers will feel it is a waste of time to offer their suggestions for product and operational improvements. Insofar as management responsive to the voices from below gives confidence to employees, such a communication gap seriously undermines any efforts at personnel education.

The tail trails the head, but the head must help the tail grow by setting a good example and by listening to the tail's side.

2. Bottom-up Communication

"HARMONY" is often thought to epitomize the pattern of human relations in Japanese organizations. I consider harmony important in a business enterprise only insofar as it provides an atmosphere conducive to a fruitful exchange of ideas and observations, which is the necessary basis for participatory management. Without harmonious relationships among employees, and between labor and management, it would be impossible to build up a fund of collective wisdom and put it to effective use.

While harmony can encourage the exchange of information and ideas, the reverse is also true. One way a company can achieve harmony is to insure a steady flow of communication from the top downwards, and vice-versa. If the thinking of the president is not conveyed to his employees, his company will not operate smoothly or efficiently, and if the aspirations and ideas of the employees are not conveyed to the top management, the company will be in even more trouble.

A person responsible for the work of many others, such as a section chief, must make sure that his staff know exactly what he is thinking. If they find some of his ideas or operating methods unacceptable, the section chief should discuss those points thoroughly with them. If the same care is taken to ensure smooth communication between the president and senior executives, between top and middle management, and between middle-echelon managers and the rank-and-file, then the company is assured of positive participation, and the collective wisdom of everyone can be fully reflected in management. Further, managers who fail to stress their thinking to the employees do so at the risk of frequent deviations from the company's basic policy line.

Far more important, however, is bottom-up communication. This is the flow of ideas and suggestions from the rank-and-file employees all the way up to the president. It is a working premise of a well-run company, and it depends heavily on middle-echelon managers. They are the ones who must encourage the staff to speak out. They are in the best position to create that all-important atmosphere in which the free exchange of opinion is taken for granted.

This kind of communication requires tremendous effort and constant attention on the part of everyone concerned. But once unimpeded, two-way communication is established and is being maintained, you will have a company managed on the basis of collective wisdom. You will have better products, better sales, and, above all, a growing enterprise with high morale among its members.

3. Bureaucratism Blocks Communication

As a company grows larger, its organization tends to grow inflexible and bureaucratic. In some extreme cases, the corporate hierarchy becomes so rigid that an employee loses direct access to anyone above him except his immediate supervisor. One may be free to approach the section chief, for example, but not the department manager. The section chief, in turn, can perhaps go straight to the department manager but is not supposed to bypass him to reach one of the directors, much less the president. Even department chiefs cannot usually go straight to the CEO.

This level of bureaucratism only prevents employees from giving free expression to their ideas, and eventually it will frustrate the company's development. Everyone, especially the officers, must always be on the alert to make sure this does not happen in their company.

The ideal business environment is one where even a freshman employee feels free to talk directly to the president if he wishes. It is the responsibility of management to create and maintain an atmosphere that encourages communication across vertical lines. The section chief, for example, can tell his employees, "It's fine with me if you wish to speak to the department manager, but give me a report later," or something similar. If an employee should bypass his immediate supervisor, this does not imply disregarding the latter's authority. When people begin to feel defensive about their own authority, the organization is already being plagued by bureaucratism.

Although the opinions or suggestions of our subordinates may not always be relevant, they may contain ideas that we never even thought of. The manager needs the ability to distinguish and apply constructive suggestions. If we are convinced that only our own ideas are valuable, we are bound by our own limitations and unable to break out in new directions. On the other hand, if we gather the wisdom of all our employees to create something new, the company will develop rapidly. To use that collective wisdom is another function of managers.

Finally, we must not give all our attention only to those suggestions that are unquestionably good, and simply toss out the others. We must hear out even those ideas that seem dubious and encourage our employees to keep thinking by asking them to try out any proposals they have. If employees believe that their supervisors are genuinely interested in their suggestions and ideas, and feel free to express themselves, their creativity will have a channel within the company, which can only benefit everyone concerned.

4. Delegate Responsibility

A basic rule to follow when assigning work is to give it to someone who wants it. In most cases, this has proven to be a reliable way to make sure the job is done well. It is not necessarily reliable, however, if ulterior motives are involved, and so you must be careful to give the job to someone who likes that kind of work and really wants to do it. It is true that, "What one likes, one will do well."

On the other hand, the execution of a job can be hampered by the inexperience or weak points of the person concerned. The manager should help that person overcome any such failings, but if there is no improvement within reasonable time, he should replace the employee. The attitude of the manager should be, "Leave it up to him, but do not abandon him to it." In other words, delegate responsibility for an assignment but do not leave the employee entirely on his own.

Final responsibility always rests with top management. Aware of this, the skillful manager will show concern for his employees' progress in the work assigned them. Although the actual work is out of his hands, it should never be out of his mind. That is why the manager should ask for regular progress reports, and if any problem arises, offer advice and instructions. This, I believe, is the principal role of a manager.

Once he delegates responsibility to someone, however, the manager does not need to interfere too much or concern himself with the small details. For the sake of the subordinate, he should leave a certain margin of tolerance. But if things start to get out of hand, the good manager is there to caution and guide. Otherwise, he is virtually abandoning those whom he himself has chosen for the task. A responsible manager would never do that.

Competent employees who are entrusted with challenging tasks will willingly submit reports or seek advice when necessary. Others will not, or only reluctantly, believing that since the work has been given to them, they should be left to do it their own way. This attitude does not contribute to the common effort, and such people should not have been selected in the first place. They should be replaced immediately.

Management depends on people, and managers must never shrug off their employees' mistakes or simply try to bear with them. As employer and employee, we must deal earnestly and punctiliously with each other. The manager's responsibility is to be constantly on the alert to make sure the right man is in the right place, at all times.

5. Rewards of Good Rapport

Procuring the necessary materials for manufacturing is by no means simply a matter of routine. It often involves touchy human issues.

Suppose a manufacturer wants to lower the price of a product by 10 percent; clearly he has to reduce his manufacturing costs proportionately, which will mean streamlining the production process. He may also have to approach the people who supply his raw materials and basic parts and try to get them to reduce their prices. This step can be difficult, and so it is crucial that the manufacturer go about it the right way.

One approach is to flatly ask for a price cut, but I personally do not think that procedure is satisfactory. I prefer to have our suppliers participate in the process. First I explain that we want to lower the price of a product by 10 percent so that more people will be able to use it, and to do that we will need their cooperation. I make a point of adding that we do not want them to lose out in any way, and I ask if they can still make a reasonable profit after lowering their price. Sometimes they reassure me that they can, in which case there is no problem, but when they say it is out of the question, I have to investigate why.

In one instance I asked a supplier to explain exactly why he could not cut his prices. His reply did not satisfy me, and so I asked to see the factory. Together we looked over the premises and considered certain areas of improvement that would allow him to lower his price without undue sacrifice. I was finally able to convince him that it was possible to reduce the price and still make a profit.

We achieved a lot more than just a price reduction. Realizing that I had considered his interests as carefully as ours, even to the point of making suggestions for him, our supplier was impressed and grateful. Knowing that we cared about his welfare motivated him further to initiate improvements on his own. Without being asked, he began to think up all sorts of improvements to cut costs and lower prices of other products. Full cooperation between manufacturer and supplier assures the prosperity of both parties. I have found that purchasing is indeed an art, and its performance depends on purely human skills—and concern.

6. An Honest Hand

A good manager should never have to resort to lies or deceit. His integrity, furthermore, will remain solid as long as he speaks the truth in every situation, even if circumstances change and he must say something quite different from what he said three months ago. Truth has a power of its own that never fails to move others, while platitudes and verbal gymnastics are irrelevant, or worse, damaging.

I am lucky that I have always been able to be truthful, and that has made it possible to do business with minimum antagonism. Situations like negotiations with the labor union are potentially very difficult, but in our company everyone always knew when the limit had been reached. I think it was because they knew that I always tried to speak the truth and to abide by it.

There is no magic in management, no clever sleights of hand. The good manager only wants to proceed with order and justice, and to win the trust of others. He is strong only when he is supported by the twin pillars of truth and trust.

An effective manager does not need a lot of knowledge, and it does not matter if he lacks dazzling technical skills. But one thing he must have is unqualified respect for the truth, and a commitment to management based on the truth. A man may get by on his knowledge or technical skills, but if that is all he has, he will never get far as a businessman. His career as a manager will stop moving long before he even approaches the top.

7. Employees Need Dreams

During my years as president of my company, I used to take any and every opportunity that arose to tell my employees about my thoughts and visions for the future. They soon learned much about what I expected of our company.

In 1956, I decided to announce to the whole company the approach we would take in our Five-Year Plan. This was unheard of and considered foolish, since it meant revealing company strategies, and thereby inviting trouble. From the management point of view, to be so open was regarded as highly improper.

Fortunately for me, my employees understood my motives. I told them that sales should increase over the next five years by so much, and actually quoted a figure. I was fully aware of the risk I took, in case this information leaked to our competitors, but I did it intentionally. First, I wanted to give my employees a chance to dream of the future and, second, I genuinely believed it was the right thing for a manager to do.

From that day on, I have always announced all my plans quite openly. The company knew right away of my intention to institute the five-day workweek (unthinkable in the early 'sixties), for example, and to pay European-scale wages. I have been criticized for my wide-open management strategy, and in some cases my critics were right—it was not well advised. But I believed that it was not right for management to give the employees only simple profit and loss figures; they should know the company's future policies and goals, also.

I feel the same way today. I think it is important to give all your employees the chance to dream. If a manager is stingy with the material of dreams, he is going to lose worker dedication and involvement in the company's future. To have dreams is to have a vested interest, a motivation. The man who can inspire a vision is a good manager.

8. Participatory Management

THE quality of management is a decisive factor in any enterprise. The best kind of management, I believe, allows all employees to participate, so that each can contribute in his own capacity to the realization of a common goal. Right from the start of my business career, I have deliberately and consistently pursued a participatory style of management.

An eloquent, competent chief executive officer may be able to guide workers toward success on the merit of his charismatic leadership alone. But I will never be convinced that a single leader, no matter how capable and powerful, can manage an organization by himself better than he could by relying on the combined wisdom of everyone on the payroll. A solitary or dictatorial style of management, depending essentially on one person, cannot last. For one reason or another, eventually it is bound to falter.

Management based on the collective wisdom of all employees sounds good, but it is not easy to put into practice; it is not easy even to explain it. Over the years, as president or chairman of Matsushita Electric, I took literally every opportunity to get the idea across that I wanted our company to be managed by all workers. I had a little lecture that went something this:

> Don't think I run this company. Each of you has a part to play in its management. We need the ideas, skill, and knowledge of everyone to make a reservoir of wisdom for more efficient operations, better product and service quality, and effective management. We have a good future if we can work that way.

It took many years, but gradually my concept of participatory management, or industrial democracy if you will, permeated the ranks of Matsushita workers. It is fair to say that management based on collective wisdom is the hallmark of all Matsushita enterprises today.

Concretely, how do you go about getting everyone involved? Is there some useful prescription or formula for soliciting and pooling ideas for common use? One method is to exchange views through meetings. Certainly a conference can provide an effective channel of communication, but too often the procedures tend either to become too formalized or to degenerate into a Babel of demagogic pronouncements or interminable rambling. In Japan where decision-making by consensus is the rule, staff meetings are particularly trying; they can go on for hours without getting anywhere.

Japanese are not adept at conducting efficient meetings or engaging in productive debate. Yet far more important than techniques or procedures, a firm commitment to participatory management on the part of all persons concerned is what makes it work. When there is a will to bring together everyone's opinions, there is a way to do so, and that ability develops with practice.

In a large corporation employing thousands or tens of thousands, it is impossible for the president to hear out each one individually. But if the president is truly committed to the ideal of participatory management, he will always make sure that the thinking and opinions of his employees reach him through different channels of intra-company communication. He must be open enough to listen to any employee, no matter what the worker's status in the corporate hierarchy. Most important of all, he must create and maintain an atmosphere in the workplace that encourages free exchange of views among employees, as well as between management and labor.

Chapter Three
Creative Management

1. Complacency Deters Progress

THERE are countless ways of management and doing business, which also means that there is unlimited room for improvement. Anything we do can almost always be done a little better. Technological innovation is a case in point. Advances are being made in leaps and bounds; breakthroughs and new inventions are occurring this very moment to make yesterday's new product out of date today. Such progress is possible only because of the belief that we can always do better.

In selling, advertising, promotion, and educating our employees, also, we can never sit back, assuming we have exhausted the options for improvement. A shop or company may be thriving, but that does not mean that it is now perfect in all its operations. Far from it! We should be constantly open to changes, ever ready to try something different, and always on the alert for new ideas in business and in management.

The process of making improvements is eternal. How it is done, or to what extent, determines whether a company will continue to develop or cease to grow. The fact that we can always do better is what makes business so exciting and fulfilling, for it means that management attitudes are directly responsible for progress.

What is important is how interested we, the managers, are. When we find something we think can be improved, either administrative or technological, or when some new development is taking place, if we get so intensely involved that even sleep seems a waste of time, we are on the right track. That is the attitude that propels growth. If, on the other hand, such events seem of little interest, then it is time to watch out. Ambivalence never achieved anything very much.

The possibilities for improvement are inexhaustible. For that reason, the ability to succeed depends in the long run on how impassioned we are in management and in business.

2. The Creative Merchant

THE job of a merchant is primarily to purchase goods from a supplier or manufacturer and sell them to the consumer as he wants or needs them. That is not all, however; the wholesale or retail merchant is also an important communicator between the consumer and the producer. He is in the best position to find out exactly what the user wants and pass that information on to the maker. The middleman can use his position to help improve the merchandise he is handling, or even generate ideas for new products.

A creative dealer gives a lot of thought to each item in his store, constantly thinking about how it might be modified to better suit the consumer's needs. He also tries to come up with innovations—new attachments, new devices, and even whole new products—and relays his ideas to the manufacturer.

Research for new product development is, of course, the manufacturer's responsibility. That is what his R & D staff and laboratory scientists are entrusted with. It may seem foolish to expect a retailer or wholesaler to contribute anything to such a highly specialized, technical task as product development, but in many cases, he can.

The retailer, in particular, is very suitably placed to receive feedback, complaints, and requests from customers. If he is truly committed to the principle of serving the consumer well, he will give serious attention to all complaints, try to analyze the reasons behind them, and work out possible solutions if he can. Once he develops some solid ideas or suggestions, the thorough retailer will take them to the manufacturer and urge him to make the necessary improvements. Through such creative initiatives the distributor can use his business, no matter how small it is, to make a really meaningful contribution to society.

American dealers and salespeople are well known for their pride in the role they play in the national economy. Many are eager to transmit the voice of the consumer to the producer. It is quite normal for them to volunteer any data and information they obtain for the benefit of the manufacturer, and to press for improvements in existing products and the development of new ones. This is the kind of creative dealership that sustains the spirit of innovation in American industry.

Is it asking too much of a retailer or dealer to initiate ideas for new merchandise or product improvements? I do not think so. I know it is easier said than done, but I also know that any such efforts are more than repaid. The real joy in business derives from the awareness that one is fulfilling important social needs by using his creativity. But the greatest rewards for any businessman are the trust of the consumer and manufacturer and the prosperity of his business.

3. Incentives for Zero Defects

An automobile company I know has a unique method of handling the invoices it receives from the various firms that supply its materials and parts. When it comes time to pay, the company always deducts a certain sum from the total bill, which it claims is for telephone charges. The initial telephone call to place the order is borne by the automobile company, but all subsequent calls, made to speed up a late delivery, for example, or complain about defective parts, are billed to the suppliers.

Another machinery company deducts a certain amount in penalty for each defective part in the delivery. The fine charged is fixed in proportion to the rate of the defects. All defective parts are returned to the suppliers, and, in addition to that, the company always deducts a fine calculated according to their percentage. Moreover, it informs the management of the supplying company, not the men in charge of delivery, about the defects and deductions made.

When I first heard about such tactics, I was very impressed, for both companies are leading firms. I wondered if they were not overdoing it, yet I admired them for their perfectionism. Then I began to see the routine logic in their approach.

Neither of those companies, I am sure, is concerned about any savings they might make by charging for telephone calls or imposing fines. Rather, their goal is simply to do away with all defects in the parts supplied, so they can manufacture top-quality products.

We cannot get rid of defective goods by constantly returning them to the supplier. That is a waste of time and effort. In the case of an automobile, especially, one defective part can affect the performance of the car itself. There are harrowing possibilities in the chance of an imperfect part, and the company must have realized the literally vital necessity of eliminating all defects. The fine, I am sure, stems from the same concern. Ultimately it is up to the supplier to eliminate defects in his products, but these are good examples of how the buyer can encourage uniform good quality through his approach to and conduct in business.

4. Intuition Makes Sense

A great many people, especially young people, dismiss intuition as unscientific, therefore unreliable. My feeling, however, is that while scientific methods can be applied in most cases, in the end we have to rely on our intuition.

I suppose I have always relied on intuition to some extent. I remain certain, in any case, that too much scientific precision is deadening, even wasteful, in my business. Some years ago, when I was chairman, I learned that our head office was requesting written reports, some daily, others monthly, from our regional sales and branch offices. When I discovered that the pile of reports had reached 240, I found it hard to believe.

I asked our sales manager why so many reports were necessary. Since they take so much time to prepare and then more time to read, I couldn't understand it. Who would read them? I could see no necessity and little use for them, and so I asked that all nonessential reports be dispensed with. The number dropped to 42.

Then there is the story about a computer we had in the 1960s, when they were still a novelty. Our office was equipped with a large computer that gave us each morning the exact sales figures for the previous day. It was a nice thing to have, but I wondered what it was costing us. I asked, and was told it was $10,000 per month, which was too much.

Right away I told our sales manager that it was a waste of money. We simply did not need to know the exact, computerized sales figures of the previous day often enough to justify the computer. It was only collecting data for its own sake. In our business, it is enough to get sales figures every five days. And, moreover, if we are doing our job and have learned to gauge the indicators, we should be able to make a close estimate of our daily sales just on intuition.

At that time, 90 percent of Matsushita Electric's sales could be estimated in that way, while the remaining 10 percent required more precise calculations. Today, of course, we need more information, and faster, than we did in the past—business methods have changed considerably to accommodate extensive office automation—but I still believe there are many occasions when intuition is valuable, and valid.

Even some of the great scientists and inventors, Thomas Edison being a case in point, relied on inspiration, and their discoveries and inventions were the result of flashes of intuition. Intuition and science are by no means incompatible. They are like the two wheels of a bicycle; when either is missing, the bicycle cannot move.

5. The Independent Spirit

THERE has been a growing tendency in recent years toward a company-based, vertical distribution system, whereby wholesalers, dealers, and retailers deal exclusively in the product lines of a single company instead of handling several brands at the same time. There are merits to the idea, and many people have adopted it.

First of all, the economy of our world is changing so quickly, and the variety of new products appearing on shop counters almost daily is so huge, that the increasing complexity of business threatens to become unmanageable. A single brand distribution system may be a good idea because it would simplify some major operations and concentrate energy, as well as reducing the risks. Furthermore, the manufacturer-wholesaler relationship and the manufacturer-retailer relationship would become closer, and customers would get better service. There is good reason to believe that such a distribution system would represent a big improvement.

Can we assume, then, that every shop or company that follows this system will be successful? Unfortunately, I think not. Whether success is achieved or not depends greatly on the ability of the man in charge, but it depends even more heavily on what I call "independent management."

When a shop handles the products of several manufacturers, the owner sees himself as his own boss. He places orders according to how he judges the market situation and his own situation. It is his shop and he buys and sells in accordance with his own ideas, and does as well as his ability will allow.

But when this man starts dealing with only one company, he begins to feel like a subsidiary of the manufacturer. With the change in his self-image goes a certain loss of management independence. For instance, if the manufacturer allocates a certain quota of goods to his shop and tells him to sell them, he will agree, even though he may think the manufacturer has overestimated the amount that can be sold. Thus he becomes totally dependent on the manufacturer. Believing that he can always return unsold stock or extend credit terms, he loses the incentive to make an all-out effort to acquire saleable goods and sell them all.

This method of management is extremely unhealthy; instead of benefitting the shop it can hurt, and hurt the consumer, too. It becomes a counterproductive system.

It will not work well unless wholesalers and retailers believe that even in dealing with a single company, they can exercise more independent management and, at the same time, work with new vigor that will benefit the consumer. Manufacturers cannot just assume that an exclusive network will improve sales. They should take it upon themselves to help wholesalers and retailers to maintain a healthy independence in management.

6. Losses Are for the Losers

OVER the years I have gotten to know many of the subcontractors who supply materials and parts to our factories. They are all different in personality and the way they think, but I have noticed something in common in all of them who are doing well. The more successful subcontractors have a degree of confidence and positiveness in their style of management that is lacking in the others.

Take, for example, their reaction when we ask them to make a price cut, in order to provide better products at lower prices. These managers never refuse outright, protesting that they will lose money. Instead they try hard to comply with our request, and react positively: "We will be happy to help make the finished product cheaper. We'll do our best, but you've got to give us another three months. We are confident that we will make it, and so please trust us."

I appreciate this sort of attitude in a subcontractor. I responded in exactly the same way when my factories were supplying parts to other companies. When asked for a price cut, I would never plead business losses as a reason not to comply. Instead, I would explain, "Well, perhaps we can make it at $5 apiece. Even $4.50 is not impossible. But since we'll have to change our methods of production here and there, we need time." Except in cases when the request was extraordinary, I always did my best to make the desired price cut. Naturally no one would have benefitted if we had tried to fulfill unreasonable demands, but when they were justified, we did our utmost to follow through.

To carry out a price cut without incurring losses, you must have the firm conviction that to lose money on any business operation is evil, and find ways to do it without financial sacrifice. If you think that you can sustain a loss here and there, then your business is bound to weaken and collapse. Such thinking amounts to defeatism, a cowardly kind of self-justification. The difference between a thriving enterprise and a teetering one lies in the philosophy of the managers concerned. A truly responsible manager starts and finishes on the assumption that business should be profitable.

7. Don't Rest on Your Laurels

Merchants in the past were extremely careful about the reputation of their enterprises. They were assiduous in cultivating the trust of their customers—and making sure that trust was justified. They worked hard to create a respected name for their shops and to sell only goods whose quality lived up to that name. To customers, the name of the enterprise signified quality, and the entrepreneur took great care to protect the name. Only those employees who had worked for him diligently and faithfully for many years were allowed to start their own businesses, using his name. These were men he judged would never hurt the reputation he had established.

That reputation developed only after constant and steady efforts exerted over many, many years of treating each customer as an important patron and providing him with good products. It was very difficult to start a business and be successful without an established name. But to begin your own business under a long-respected name assured you of success.

The world of commerce is somewhat different today. The importance given to good credit and to the treatment of customers has remained the same, but in our rapidly changing society, an enterprise cannot survive on reputation alone. In the past, even when there was a lapse in the performance of a business, its reputation would probably compensate. This is no longer true. No matter how old and respected its name may be, a business today will receive no quarter if it demonstrates incompetence or inadequacy in its performance. It will eventually go under.

A reputation that has been built up over many years is still important, of course, but when it collapses, it collapses overnight, just like a doomed building. Perhaps it took a year to construct, but only a few days are enough to tear it down.

It is wise to remember that credit already earned is not as reliable in business as it once was. The successful entrepreneur has to be constantly up to date on what customers want, and he must make sustained efforts to meet every new need, thus earning new credit, day by day.

8. Business Shapes Society

PERHAPS no era has seen more constant, rapid change than our own, and no manager with his wits about him can fail to see that management must keep abreast of the times, just to survive. Companies that continue to use the same old management techniques have a very bleak future. Truly competent managers attuned to the ever-changing present, on the other hand, are in a position to help shape a new epoch.

As with every decade, the 1980s has its share of futurologists who bombard us with forecasts. Statesmen, too, are concerned with the future, but their approach is different. While futurologists are analysts, using data from the past and present to predict the future, statesmen, ideally, are builders who envision a better society in the future and try to recreate their vision in reality.

Today's managers can contribute more by creating a vision and working toward it, like statesmen, than acting on the basis of analyzed data. Surely all businessmen, working hard day after day, have hopes and ideals. They should share their hopes with their employees and together work toward realizing them. That means continually sizing up all the factors that affect one's work and making a reasonable assessment of the situation he will face in a year or two. In such uncertain times, this is particularly important because we can take so little for granted.

I, myself, have always tried to look ahead, and I always made a point of sharing my visions with my employees. Together we succeeded in realizing many of them. This, I believe, is one of the main reasons for the solid progress of Matsushita Electric. In the process, moreover, I learned that there are limits; to pursue our visions too relentlessly, or push our own ideas too persistently, is counterproductive.

The best approach is to keep an open mind, judge matters accurately, and proceed one step at a time in the unfailing belief that business is responsible for shaping a new epoch. To me, flexible, positive moderation is an important element for success in our restless times.

Chapter Four
Spirit of Service

1. The Unwritten Contract

It is standard practice among many manufacturers and dealers to conduct business on the basis of firm advance orders. The majority of Japanese businesses, however, operate without any advance orders, and the consumer simply buys what he needs from what is available on the market at any given time. My own company works that way, and a large part of our annual sales of US$15 billion made on the open market involves no advance orders.

Practically speaking, it is unreliable and risky to conduct business on the basis of estimates rather than orders. When there is no definite commitment, there is no guarantee of being able to sell all of what you produce. And you can only blame yourself when stock remains unsold.

There is no simple way to reach the right balance and produce the necessary quantity without having stock left over or running out too soon, but there are certain principles that seem to work. If they are followed, you cannot go too far wrong.

There are no signed agreements, but a company does have unwritten contracts with the people who buy its products. They can buy its goods freely, whenever they wish. I think of that demand as an unwritten contract, since it obliges the supplier to produce what the consumers want. To fulfill that demand is the sole clause in his contract with the people.

The same applies when you wish to increase production or sales, expand your facilities, or buy new equipment. If you do all this with a sense of obligation to the consumers, the whole company benefits. Although no one has placed an actual order with you, still you know they want your products. This I take to mean an advance order, a "contract." The next step is to fulfill your terms. This approach generates a surge of confidence, and a powerful new vitality appears in your business.

My perception of this unwritten contract has guided my business operations from the start. It has always let me supply the consumers with what they want without over- or under-production.

International business grows more complicated each day, and the complexities of producing and selling continue to multiply. But underneath the intricate problems of manufacturing and trade, this unwritten contract and the manufacturers' responsibility to consumers remain basic constants. If you fully recognize those constants and respond fully, your business will be solidly grounded.

2. Advertising Is Evangelizing

It is the manufacturer's role, his very raison d'être, to make quality products that people find useful and beneficial. His job involves a lot more, however; he must also inform the public fully about his products. With each new product, the maker is obligated to explain to the consumer how it will help improve daily life. That is what advertising is. The real purpose is not so much to push sales as to bring good news to people. In this sense, advertising is very much like an evangelical mission.

Advertising also serves to stimulate the activities of retailers and wholesalers and promote their sales. The dealer's role is to distribute to users, directly or indirectly, good-quality merchandise supplied by the manufacturer. If the manufacturer neglects his duty to advertise, thinking that sales promotion is not his job, the distributor will feel he is not getting the moral support he needs, and sales will suffer. On the other hand, the manufacturer's active interest in advertising will boost the sales force and raise morale, giving them greater confidence and enthusiasm in their work.

Industry today depends heavily on advertising and sales promotion, and I would be the last to criticize the emphasis on these activities. More often than not, however, advertisements seem to be directed only at increasing sales. Too many of them give exaggerated or misleading images of the products. When that happens, the ad is no longer a source of information, and it is certainly not "good news," for it leads to disappointment. I think all of us in manufacturing should periodically review our ads, and never forget the original purpose they are meant to serve.

3. Service Comes First

AFTER-SALES service is the key to keeping your customers. No matter how good the product you put on the market, if you do not provide equally good after-sales service, the customer will not come back. He will shower you with complaints and then go elsewhere. In many respects service is more important than the product itself. If you cannot provide good after-sales service for all the products you offer, you should consider reducing your range, from five product lines to three, for example. In the long run, it is better to reduce the scale of business and achieve perfection in the quality *and* servicing of a smaller number of products. A manufacturer who cannot do that much defaults on his responsibility toward his customers.

Therefore, whenever you consider expanding operations you must first ask yourself if you can fulfill that responsibility—i.e., if you can provide good service. Only if the answer is yes, should you go ahead. If you do not have full confidence in your ability to provide satisfactory servicing, you should not expand at that time. If you do, regardless of any success the new operation may have at first, unsatisfactory after-sales service will alienate the customers. At worst, it could bring your whole business down.

Products, sales, and service are an inseparable trio. A successful business makes a contribution, and that contribution lies in good service. Good business needs good products, but more, good service. With that, a business can develop to its maximum potential.

4. "Hello" Service

AFTER-SALES service is going to become important from now on, as the number of sophisticated devices on the market that would require a specialist to repair or adjust can only increase. It has already been found that the store which places equal emphasis on sales and after-sales service flourishes.

After-sales service is especially effective if you act *before* the customer complains about your product or something goes wrong with it. For example, when summer approaches and people take out their electric fans, just drop in at the houses of customers who bought fans at your store last year. Say "hello," and ask how the fan is working, then check the fan and clean it. I call this "hello" service.

The service is free, of course. There is no immediate profit. But the customer is pleased and his or her trust in you goes up by a large percentage. For a businessman, there is no greater happiness and sense of worth in your work than what your customers' delight and their trust in you can give.

But free after-sales service, even before it is requested, demands extraordinary effort and investment. If you run a retail store, you yourself must first be convinced that "hello" service is necessary, and then convince your employees. Keep stressing why it is so important until they really understand it and are glad to make the rounds. Then your store will most certainly thrive. Your products should give no trouble, for, since you and your employees know the importance of service, you will naturally be careful to show the customer how to use a product properly when he buys it from you. And after-sales service will ensure that the product remains in good working condition. You will get fewer complaints from your customers, and they will be pleased with what you sold them. After-sales service requires close cooperation among retail store, wholesaler, and maker, but the role of the retailer, the direct link to the customers, is primary.

After a daughter marries, her parents worry and wonder if she is getting along with her husband and the in-laws. A product from your store is like a married daughter. Do not forget about it, keep it in mind, and wonder how it is doing. Think about the customer, too, who has, after all, become something like a relative. And check up from time to time by giving "hello" service.

5. Persuasion Pays Off

A good businessman knows how to be persuasive. Suppose a customer comes into your shop and says, in exasperation, "How come you give only a 10 percent discount when other stores are taking 15 percent off?" How would you handle him? If you give in to pressure from him, you will lose your profit margin, which, for a businessman, is like digging your own grave. On the other hand, if you flatly refuse any further markdown, you risk losing a customer for good.

This is where the art of persuasion comes into play. You must somehow convince the unhappy customer that your price is indeed reasonable. In your own style, you might say something like the following: "This is really the best price we can offer you without cutting our own throats. At this price, though, we will guarantee the best after-sales service, as prompt and complete as you can get."

Persuasiveness is just as important in religion. A religion has to capture the hearts of all kinds of people if it is to gain a significant following. Of course it must also have a solid doctrinal base, but no matter how compelling the tenets, if the sect itself lacks the appeal, the ability to win sympathy, it will not grow. This is perhaps even more true in the mundane world of business because you are dealing with more tangible goods and services, and you are expected to comply with the highly diverse, specific needs of consumers.

More than anything else, you need confidence in the quality of the products or services you are selling, and, of course, in their value to consumers. Your commodities must also be reasonably priced. If those conditions are fulfilled, you have a strong advantage. If you still cannot sway your customers, I would suspect that you are not really cut out for business. Or perhaps you are in the wrong kind. A misplaced businessman can do little for himself or anyone else—customers, shareholders, patrons, suppliers, or whoever. If the power of persuasion is a meaningful measure of entrepreneurship, you had probably better take a good, hard look at yourself in terms of your own persuasiveness, for it is self-confidence and competence that make a good businessman.

6. Good Quality, Good Price

IF you watch and listen, you can learn a lot from other peoples' experiences. I certainly have. In one case, for example, a Japanese company wanted to get into the West German market and sent one of its senior executives there for negotiations. The quality of their products was high, and so the Japanese side, confident of their international competitiveness, decided to approach a top German wholesaler. The executive and the wholesaler began to work out terms, but when they came to pricing, they ran into a snag.

The Japanese remarked that he would like to sell his products at prices comparable to those of top-quality, reputable, German products. At this, the other man balked. "That would be way too high!" he protested. "Other Japanese companies keep their prices 15 percent lower here. You can't price yours at the same level with top-class German products. We won't be able to sell them."

In the mid-fifties this was a perfectly understandable reaction. Yet the Japanese executive replied, "Our products are the same as, if not better than, those made here in Germany. Doesn't it stand to reason that our prices should also be the same? But our products do differ from yours in one way—they are not known here. So if we want them to sell we need you also to explain to German consumers that these are indeed first-class products. For that reason, we propose to lower the price by 3 percent, if only for a promotional effect."

On that basis, they reached an agreement. The German wholesaler was satisfied, and commented that it was the first time he had met a Japanese businessman who actually taught him something. He added, "Now I know a little more about what business means. I am happy to sell your products."

This anecdote was extremely interesting to me, for it meant that while some Japanese companies were selling their products for 15 percent less, another was selling at the same price as comparable German products, less a 3 percent promotion fee. Moreover, the products sold extremely well. Until then, the prices of Japanese goods had fluctuated wildly; what was first priced at DM10 was later reduced to DM9 and then to DM8. But undercutting only served to undermine confidence in Japanese products, causing a lot of lost sleep for the wholesalers handling them. In this case there was no such anxiety, and as confidence in the products rose, they sold better than those of their Japanese competitors.

7. Treasure Complaints

DURING my long tenure as president and chairman, I frequently received letters from consumers, sometimes praising our products, but, more often, finding fault with them. Naturally I liked getting letters of praise, but I was even more grateful for the complaints.

In one case, we received a letter from a professor, complaining that a product we had supplied his university was not working properly. I immediately sent the man in charge of that product to the university. The professor was in an ugly mood, but when our man explained what was wrong and proceeded to correct it, the professor forgot his anger. In a warm, friendly way, he even suggested other departments in the university that might buy the same product. The fact that the professor had complained and we had dealt with the problem brought us new business.

That is why complaints are valuable; they give an opportunity to establish direct contact with customers. Those who do not complain probably come to the decision never to buy that company's products again. Those who do complain might think the same thing at first, but if you take the trouble to visit them and take care of their complaint, they appreciate your sincerity. Thus, depending on how you handle grievances, you might end up with a fan instead of a critic.

Of course, if you sit back and make no response to complaints you receive, or if you handle them badly, you may end up with dwindling customers. For that reason, every time you are reproached by consumers, look for the possibility of a closer business relationship. Treat your customers with respect, look for and understand the cause of their dissatisfaction, and tackle it in earnest. The worst thing to do is to ignore a complaint. Rather, make the best use of an opportunity at hand.

8. Loyal Subjects

When I went to Europe for the first time in 1951, I met the president of a large European company, who, in the course of conversation, remarked, "You know, Mr. Matsushita, I look at it this way: the consumer is king and our company is a loyal subject always ready to serve the king. Therefore, whatever our king—the consumer—demands, we have to accommodate him, no matter how difficult. That is our duty, and the basic principle behind our activities."

Today the phrase, "the consumer is king," is common, but it certainly wasn't then, over thirty years ago. It had a fresh ring to it and I was impressed by the truth and perception it contained.

At the same time, another thought occurred to me. Time and again in history we have seen how, when a king neglects his subjects, eventually they lose their desire to work and end up in serious straits. Sometimes the kingdom itself declines or is vanquished. It is one thing to obey the king, for that is the duty of every subject, but shouldn't subjects who are truly loyal also inform him when he is on the wrong track?

Perhaps loyalty takes two forms. One way of expressing it is to obey the king's every wish, even to the point of absurdity. The other way—what I consider true loyalty—is to give the king proper advice when he is misled, even at the risk of angering him. Subjects who are genuinely loyal are concerned enough to want to help their king act with prudence and wisdom.

The consumer-king is stronger today, which is all to the good. But it is that much more important that we remember the role of the loyal subject—to help the king make the right decisions. Then, together, the wise ruler and his loyal subjects can seek the prosperity of their society and nation. We must remember that "the consumer is king," but that his sovereign responsibility goes far beyond simply giving order.

Chapter Five
Social Responsibility

1. The Public Eye

THE phrase "the public eye" means different things to different people. To me, it evokes the idea of an arbiter, a judge of right or wrong, fair or unfair. I have faith in the judgment of the people, and I believe their verdict is ultimately sound. To be able to trust their collective judgment is very important in business. It allows you to move ahead positively and with conviction, assured of a reliable, ever-present standard.

If the people were erratic in their basic attitudes and unreliable in judgment, there would be times when they would fail to appreciate, or even reject, the most ethical business practices. An erratic public would make it impossible to conduct business with the necessary confidence, no matter how conscientious you tried to be. Even after years of operation, if you were constantly anxious about how people reacted to your products, pricing policy, sales methods, or promotional efforts, you would not be able to give the wholehearted attention your business itself required.

Fortunately, "the public eye" is steadfast. I know from long experience that the public, or society, supports anyone who conducts his business sensibly, rationally, and fairly. As long as your practices conform with accepted business norms, your enterprise is on solid ground. If something goes wrong, you may have veered off track and should reexamine your own conduct before blaming your customers, the consumers, or anyone else. If you have faith in the essential truth of popular wisdom and can accept the dictates of the people's judgment, it will be easy to correct your mistakes and make adjustments when necessary. Dynamic, flexible management is vital for a business, but it is possible only when you have broad public support behind you.

I may sound naively optimistic in my basic trust of the public, and I grant that, indeed, "The world has as many fools as wise men." History is filled with episodes of good trampled on by evil, right overwhelmed by wrong, and justice pushed aside by injustice. Conversely, how many times is the good, earnest, constructive person relegated to obscurity, sometimes dying in pain and humiliation. Probably no society can escape the stigma of frequent injustice and wrong in its history.

Even conceding that, however, I am still convinced that in the long run the people pass the correct judgment on what is right and what is wrong. Without that conviction, where would we ever find a sense of security? On what could we base our hopes for the future? It is this fundamental optimism that allows us to make a deep commitment to our work and to the fulfillment of our ideals.

2. The Businessman's Right to Profit

In business it is of the utmost importance to aim at a fair profit. Only by making a reasonable profit—neither too much nor too little—can an enterprise expand and be of greater service to more people. Moreover, the enterprise contributes to society by paying a large portion of its profits in the form of taxes. In that sense, it is a businessman's duty, as a citizen, to make a reasonable profit.

The rationale of business is, of course, to make available good-quality, reasonably-priced goods to fulfill the needs of the consumers. We must, therefore, be constantly on the lookout for new ways of making better products, as well as devising more effective sales methods and offering better service. At the same time, we should always try to make a fair profit. Dumping, over-competition, and other such practices ultimately confound the efforts of everyone in the industry.

In trying to make a reasonable profit, we should always remember the importance of reducing unnecessary expenses as much as possible. To that end, everyone from the top down must be cost-conscious, to the point of saving money on phone calls, stationery, and so forth. A reasonable profit should be the result of constant efforts to raise efficiency and reduce costs.

Even if businessmen agree on the necessity for fair profit, the consumers, the general public, need to be convinced. They need to be told that our profits, which, of course, affect the price, are not made for profits' sake. We must take every opportunity to impress them with the importance of profits as a source of society's prosperity, and the means by which our enterprises can serve them better. With patience and perseverance, it can be done. Convincing people to accept reasonable profits is a key to creating a business environment that will bring real benefits to society.

3. Mind Your Business

To do business well, it is very important to conduct yourself and your company in ways that will support its prosperity in the future. As a manager, you must be serious, which means giving punctilious care to the smallest details. The payment and collection of bills may seem too trivial for a manager to worry about, but they are at the heart of financial viability, and so it is surprising how often they are neglected.

In the case of bankruptcy, while it frequently stems from causes beyond the company's control, it is also true that stricter management could have prevented it. Inattention over a long period to the tedious, but vital day-to-day chores, such as settling accounts, can be fatal. That neglect is not intentional, but when the people in charge become so obsessed with selling that they forget about the accounts, financial problems are bound to occur.

It is not only small or medium enterprises that are guilty of slack management. Even large firms have a tendency to neglect details. At first it doesn't show, but then the company starts running into trouble, which snowballs until the decline is literally irreversible.

When we become sloppy in money matters, we become sloppy about everything else. You will find that shops and companies that are in the black are also very careful about all money matters, including paying and collecting bills. Regardless of the size of a business, if you want to manage it well and keep it going, you cannot afford to be sloppy.

It is good to recall the story of the wholesaler with a middle-sized business who, even in difficult times, managed to make a healthy profit. He was greatly liked and trusted by all his suppliers and retailers alike. His secret was to be precise about payment and collection of bills and, as a consequence, exact and punctual in all aspects of his business. In other words, his approach to business was serious and precise, and slowly he built up a large reservoir of trust among those he dealt with. The important factor behind prosperity may well lie in nothing more than this simple attitude toward one's job.

4. No Compromise

In doing business, if you do it right, there is no such thing as compromise. In other words, whatever the job, make sure that it is completely satisfactory before you let it out of your hands.

Suppose your manufacturing company has just received a large order for a certain type of product with specifications. You know that the quality of that product does not meet your standards, but if you do not accept it, you may not get another order later on. What should you do?

Most of us, when confronted with this situation, would probably be tempted to take the easy way out; we would supply the product, vowing never to compromise again. That is understandable for it is all too human. But this is actually a crucial decision. It marks a point after which your business will either succeed or fail. At this point, you must not give in to human weakness.

It is essential to be determined to let no product ever leave the factory floor until you are completely satisfied with its quality, no matter whose order it is. You should also make certain all your employees have the same determination.

Acting on conviction, we must try to attain perfection in all we do. Of course, real perfection in this world is impossible, but nonetheless, unless we have this basic promise to ourselves, we will not be able to handle our company when it begins to expand and its products diversify and multiply.

One company I know is very successful, largely because both its management and workers will not tolerate compromise. They never permit any goods to leave the factory unless their quality is wholly satisfactory, and they make no exceptions no matter what type of order it is or who it comes from. This company is not afraid of competitors. As long as they maintain quality and are punctual, they know no one will take their business away.

Tenacity of purpose does not equal inflexibility. Wise management is always prepared to consider alternate modes of action when necessary. This, then, is the basic approach one needs to do the kind of work in which he can take pride and deliver with confidence.

5. Fair Competition for Progress

THERE is no point in economic competition for its own sake. It is a means to achieve worthy objectives that are far more important than the process of competing itself. But healthy competition in business is an asset. It encourages industry and innovation and it motivates people to improve their work performance. Just as monopoly causes stagnation, competition nurtures progress.

When it goes too far, on the other hand, competition can be counterproductive. In excess, it disrupts the market and ultimately erodes the prosperity of the industry concerned. Consumers, firms in adjacent or related industries, financial institutions, and everyone else with direct or indirect interests in the industry will suffer when rivalry gets out of hand.

Whether manufacturer, distributor, or retailer, anyone involved in competition must keep his tactics clean and fair. No one should ever try, or be allowed to try, to outdo his competitors by exploiting political influence, for example, or push smaller firms out of business simply by manipulating his greater financial power. Transgressions like that lead to anarchy, and then the whole industry is doomed.

In fair competition, the companies concerned contend on the basis of product quality and service: the firm that performs best in both areas comes out ahead. Radical price cutting—dumping—does nothing but disservice to the customer in the long run. Nor is it fair to try to force one's way into a bigger share of the market at the expense of the others.

Preoccupation with self-interest and lack of concern for the stability and prosperity of the industry as a whole are twin factors behind unfair, excessive competition. Whether you are dealing with a particular industry, a community or the nation, the most important thing to remember is to consider the good of the whole. In the end, your own interests are most secure when the interests of everyone are served.

6. Survival of the Competent

A laissez-faire economy and competition go hand in hand. Competition encourages dedicated work, and hard work is what builds a better society. Thus, it is all the more important that competition be fair, based not on power, but on something with more lasting value.

I am talking about a moral code, an ethic, that provides a standard for right and wrong. Such a code should dictate how we conduct our activities, for without it, society would become the domain of the powerful, determined only by those with brute strength on their side. The rule of power does not bring prosperity; quite the contrary, history has shown time and again that power, unchecked, leads to violence.

Fair competition allows even small companies with little capital an equal chance of success based on management competence and efficiency. It is hard to measure competence in specific terms, but certainly conscience, diligence, and a flair for creativity are important elements. Those are qualities one can develop without great wealth or influence and if competition revolves around them, anyone with genuine ability can do well in any area of business.

On the other hand, if financial power decides the rules of competition, then skills become less important, and small companies with little capital but able managers will never be competitive. No one benefits, in the long run, when financial clout is the determining factor, neither society nor the companies concerned.

In manufacturing, each firm should use all its inventiveness and originality to produce quality goods—keeping costs and overhead down for lower retail prices—and make a reasonable profit. That is what leads to progress, and competition in this sense should be encouraged. When the terms of competition are fair, even smaller companies can compete on equal ground with larger ones. Given a competent manager, a small or medium-sized firm is even better suited for dynamic competition.

In any case, those who are cut out for one field will survive the competition, while those who are not should seek to fulfill their potential in other areas. This, to me, is a natural pattern of progress, and is essential to the development of a well-balanced society.

7. Two Sides of Affluence

THE role of business and industry is to respond to the needs of people and to improve the quality of their lives by producing and distributing the widest variety of goods possible. Essentially, business exists to help raise their standard of living.

We do not live by bread alone, however; possessing material

comforts in no way guarantees happiness. Only spiritual wealth can bring true happiness. If that is true, should business be concerned only with the material aspect of life and leave the care of the human spirit to religion or ethics? I do not think so. Businessmen, too, should be able to share in creating a society that is spiritually rich and materially affluent.

One thing we can do is to establish sound business practices and ethics and to try and uphold them. For instance, if we are slack in settling accounts, our business tends to become sloppy. That, in turn, can have a demoralizing effect on those involved, and by extension, on the whole community. Thus, we have to be punctilious in handling our finances and encourage others to be equally conscientious about the remittance and collection of payments.

It is no exaggeration to say that healthy business begins with punctual settlement of accounts. A firm or store operated on a financially and ethically solid footing will have a positive effect on everyone associated with it, be they employees or customers. Some will even sense a morally uplifting, beneficial influence within themselves in the course of its operation.

Another important service the business community can and should perform for the spiritual fulfillment of people is to encourage independence in management. Constant efforts to cut down on borrowing and to augment equity capital, to improve the quality of products or services through internal R & D, and to solve whatever problems that may arise with one's own resources, not at the expense of others—all these illustrate what I call independent management. The business community should encourage all managers to pursue policies and activities that will enhance corporate autonomy, and it should promote cooperation among businessmen in the spirit of entrepreneurial independence. If the business community can succeed in these efforts, it will be an exemplary sector of society.

I am sure that there are many other ways in which business and industry can contribute to the spiritual enrichment of people's lives. The most basic corporate responsibility to society, however, is for each enterprise to stand on its own feet. Only then can corporations, both small and large, begin to work toward building a truly affluent society, affluent in both its spiritual and material life.

8. An Era for Political Concern

For everyone except the very young, the world today is far removed from the world of yesterday. For the businessman who has known slower, less complex times, it is hard to avoid the uneasy, intimidating feeling that somehow, no matter what he does, he has lost control of his destiny.

In the not-too-distant past, business and politics were separate realms, and businessmen could carry on without having to worry much about politics. Today, business and politics are virtually interwoven; there is almost no way an enterprise can escape the heavy influence of politics on its policies and performance. Given a solidly directed national and international environment, this might be all right, but such is not the case. We find ourselves up against the muddled confusion of politics in Japan, and unable to extricate ourselves, regardless of what efforts we make. We end up only compounding our problems, unable to keep them in check.

Most people will agree that the nation's objectives are ill-defined; the vacillations of our political leaders leave the business community, as well as the general public, wondering what is coming next. All of us hope that in time some clear-cut objectives will emerge for Japan. That will make management much easier. But the point is that they haven't yet, and until they do, people in business must do their best to make decisions and act, within our own limits, in ways that we think will most benefit our society and enable us to prosper.

Regardless of the status of our national policy, we should determine the direction of our business according to our own best judgment. Difficulties may abound, but we have to create our own philosophy and have the conviction to do what we judge to be right. It is important to develop business ideals and share them with one another, for the sharing of a vision helps to create stability, progress, and singleness of purpose.

As businessmen and as members of society, we are also responsible for conveying our opinions, firmly and constructively, to politicians regarding the policies that we think will benefit the nation most. We cannot, today, expect to gain greater stability in the business sector without actively concerning ourselves with what politicians are saying and thinking. The business-and-politics approach may seem a gratuitous infringement on our sphere of activity, but if all of us care enough to try, one day a consensus on national policy may emerge, giving greater security to the world of business.

Chapter Six

Challenge and Growth

1. Trouble Is a Good Teacher

TROUBLES and dilemmas are routine in business. Sometimes we can cope, other times we are truly confounded. In an impasse, the first step is to remain calm and rational.

For me, a very important way of handling a serious situation is to reflect—honestly and without prejudice—on the situation and why it happened. It may have been beyond my power to avoid it, but chances are just as good that the cause had something to do with me. For anyone, it is all too easy to miscalculate or mishandle an important matter. When that happens, one must face his error honestly. A way out will emerge if he tries to find it, and the experience will be an invaluable lesson.

Ultimately, through failure we achieve wisdom, and defeat provides a valuable fund of experience to draw from later on. Failure also gives us useful insights into ourselves and our circumstances. From it, we can grow and progress.

There is no successful businessman who has not at some time or other encountered failure. And with each such experience, he gains some wisdom or insight, and he matures a little more. Confidence and success are built on that base of experience.

That is why, each time we find ourselves in a difficult situation of our own making, the only satisfatory solution is to face it squarely and admit our error. If we do not, we will learn nothing, no matter how often the same difficulty crops up. Laying the blame on someone else will only compound it. Recognizing the cause of failure and reminding ourselves that it was a good, if expensive, lesson, we will be that much stronger for it.

2. Living on a Tightrope

OUR era has been dubbed the "Age of Uncertainty," and uncertain it is. Nowadays it is well-nigh impossible to predict very much with accuracy. This only compounds the problems of a company president or manager, who already has more than enough to cope with. Still, this is nothing new. We have faced it before and we will face it again.

A person with strong motivation is actually challenged in our bewildering times, stimulated to use all his skills to overcome odds and come out stronger than before. But others are disturbed and confused by their inability to impose order on their world. This type of manager will never be able to lead his company to prosperity. A manager with longevity must be prepared to weather storms and face unruly situations, undaunted.

It used to be said that a samurai had to be ready to deal with seven foes lying in wait whenever he left his house. He was trained to be prepared to meet death at every corner, and it was this readiness that earned him admiration and respect.

The manager today needs to be even more prepared than the samurai. He must always be conscious of the possibility that his business or he, himself, could topple at any time, as if he were walking a very dangerous tightrope. This is not the time for a relaxed, nonchalant outlook on life or business. The serious manager must keep alert to dangers and his responsibilities even when he is enjoying himself at a party. If he can stay alert and still enjoy socializing, then he is a skillful manager. If he is alert but anxious, then he should not be playing the part of manager.

A president is charged with the guidance of each and every one of his employees. If he has ten thousand employees, his concern for them has ten thousand faces. Sleep does not come easily and his troubles weigh heavily. Yet the sleepless nights and concern are also what make his life worthwhile. There has never been a company president who has had no worries. Worry and heavy responsibility are part and parcel of the job.

3. Recession Academy

HUMAN nature never ceases to make me wonder. When everything is going well, we tend to become lax. Particularly at such times we must remind ourselves of the proverb, "In fair weather prepare for foul." Times of prosperity give the leeway to make preparations for possible adversity, but in fact, people have short memories.

When the going is good, we quickly forget the bad times until they are upon us again. Caught unprepared, we grow anxious. We tell ourselves that somehow things will turn out all right, and extra effort will pull the business out of its slump. That is the way we develop as businessmen and as human beings, and it is at such adverse times that this development takes place.

The same is true of our employees. They do not develop as much in the trouble-free periods of prosperity as during times of difficulty. Naturally I do not encourage making an effort to invite troubles—that would be senseless. It is more important that our company function smoothly. But I still believe that periods of recession or slumps offer the best opportunity for training personnel. No one welcomes a recession, and in principle, we should be able to control or eliminate them. In reality, however, the economy is such today that a boom is inevitably followed by a slack period.

When business is bad, sales are sluggish, bills are difficult to collect, and everyone is constricted by financial problems. This is no time for grumbling; at such times we should be thinking positively about how to give a real-life education to our employees. And as long as we have the will to ride it out, there is no time like a slump to educate our employees and to strengthen our management. It all depends on one's attitude.

4. Pitfalls of Deficit Financing

A sure sign of hard times is the large number of bankruptcies sprinkled throughout the news. What amazes me, however, is the size of the debts these companies run up. Before World War II, if a company capitalized at, say, $20,000, collapsed with a debt two or three times that figure, it was a sensational news. But today, it is not at all unusual for a company of equivalent size to end up with a debt twenty to thirty times its paid-in capital.

This strikes me as extremely unhealthy, and a sign of weakness in the economy and values of modern Japan. When conditions are good, those companies can manage, but the moment money supply becomes tight, they are in trouble and business grinds to a halt.

The practice of overborrowing probably developed in the immediate postwar years, when companies had lost all their assets and property and were forced to rely heavily on outside funds. But things are very different today. Money is not scarce, and any company that can afford to incorporate should be able to manage with the funds it has in hand. It should stay within its means.

In practice, I know how difficult this is. You cannot get along on your own funds until you have earned enough to begin with. And you cannot do that simply by marking up your retail prices, because cheaper competition would take away all your customers. The only way is to streamline your operations and lower your overhead and direct expenses, while giving your customers the best after-sales service. If you can do that much, you will not only satisfy your customers but also be assured of a reasonable profit. Your business will stay afloat and eventually prosper.

A huge debt left after bankruptcy has to be paid by someone. You can lighten the burden on others by your own financial self-reliance. If you are really determined, you can find ways to do that.

5. Give Yourself Leeway

NOWADAYS Japanese banks almost always make a loan conditional upon a fixed savings deposit, in addition to collateral. At one time this was a controversial issue because both the government and the Bank of Japan regarded it as a somewhat dubious practice, but today it is routine.

For a half-century, however, I have made it a habit to make just this kind of deposit, even if the bank did not request it. Whenever I got a loan, I would borrow twice as much as I needed and put half the sum into a fixed deposit. Invariably I sustained a loss each time, simply because the interest I paid on the loan was much higher than what I earned on the fixed deposit. But I did not think of it as a loss, only as insurance—capital in reserve that I could use for emergencies. The bank manager trusted me and fully approved of the cautious way I handled loans, even without suggestions from the bank. Most important, I never worried about not having enough when I borrowed money because I knew I could always draw on the extra amount I had borrowed and deposited. Whatever losses I absorbed, I am certain they were compensated in the end. Laying aside an emergency reservoir is what I call "dam management."

Dam management is just as necessary in other areas of business. You really should have a personnel dam, an equipment dam, an inventory dam, a technology dam, and so on. It is wise to establish such reserves in every sector of your business, just to ensure that you will never be left high and dry. Dam management is not directly profitable nor is it technically essential. But it is a very useful practice for enterprises whose aim is long-term stability and development.

It can also be seen as the principle of limited response. If the maximum weight you can lift is fifty pounds, you should never carry more than forty pounds. If you take on the maximum weight, you will likely trip or fall over. The ten-pound margin of safety cuts the risk of an accident. In other words, be moderate. If you work at 80 percent of your capacity, you will always have 20 percent in reserve to deal with emergencies, such as a sudden increase in demand.

Mind you, business should always yield a profit, even when it is run by dam management principles. The essential factor is an accurate estimate of market conditions. Suppose you estimate demand for a certain product at 100. To produce 80 is over-cautious, so you had better make it 90. You should never make it 100, because if the estimate is even a little too high, you will end up with unsold stock.

What is important here is to make the correct estimate in the first place. Do not make the mistake of guessing 120, or

80, when the level of demand is 100—either one will lead you into trouble. Dam management can be effective only when your initial estimates are correct.

6. Earthquake Shakeup

In 1964 a big earthquake hit Niigata on the Japan Sea coast. It destroyed buildings, bridges, and caused an enormous amount of damage to the city and its people, as well as to business and financial institutions. Our company had a sales office in Niigata, and so I expected certain losses, but from the reports I received, the amount we lost was out of proportion to the level of office we maintained.

If we had had a factory in the region, a loss of that size would have been understandable, but for a sales outlet it was too high. Gradually I learned that more goods than were required had been sent to Niigata, and not being sold, they had just accumulated there as excess stock. Had the proper amount of goods been sent and optimum inventory maintained, we would not have lost so much.

In general, when a natural disaster brings losses, people tend to accept it as fate. This is especially true of earthquakes, since we have no reliable system to predict when one is about to hit. An earthquake is recognized as a natural disaster and considered inevitable. In fact, although an earthquake is indeed an act of fate, the size of your loss is by no means inevitable. It is directly proportionate to your skill at management.

After the Niigata experience, I decided to check all our regional sales offices and discovered similar situations in several other places. I set out to do something about it. My staff discussed various approaches, and finally agreed on a rationalization plan. Without the earthquake, we would never have noticed what was going on in the sales offices, but as it was, we were given the chance to find problems and make necessary adjustments, and we benefitted by them. The earthquake caused terrible suffering, but recouping afterwards, for me and others, was a stimulating challenge for management.

7. Events of an Uneventful Day

THE accumulation of experience that each day brings, as we all know, is an important part of business. Both failures and successes remain with us as valuable lessons. The events that punctuate a business career are our lifeblood, so to speak, and the older a person gets, the more experience he has gained. That quality shows in his work, and merits respect, for he has learned as the years go on. Without experiencing either success or failure, the passage of time is meaningless.

Most of us value experience, but few realize how much is learned not only from success or failure, but from routine events as well. Even days that seem dull and uneventful can teach us something.

Actually, it seems to me, the small things are quite important. Each detail during the day that demands a decision can be evaluated in terms of failure or success. The big failures are debts, late deliveries, bankruptcies, etc., but we encounter many other failures, too. In fact, there is no such thing as absolute failure or absolute success. Rather, in the ramifications of every failure are partial successes, and there is no success without some elements of failure in it.

At the end of an uneventful day, the careful manager takes

stock of all his actions and decisions that day to assess how far he succeeded or failed. He asks himself what, among them, he should have handled better, and whether a given solution was really the best. It is a process of analytical reflection that adds up to very useful experience, even on humdrum days.

There is much to be learned even in working out the trivial mistakes that occur daily, unnoticed by most other people. The challenge is to turn those mistakes into useful experience. If we wander haplessly through each day, without reflection, we will grow old without having gained the maturity that worthwhile experience brings.

Managers are duty-bound to share their experience and to make sure that their employees have the chance to learn from their own. If they do not give their employees the responsibility for certain tasks or projects, and if they do not encourage them to think for themselves, the employees, at worst, will be like robots, responding only to orders when a button is pushed.

That is an inhuman way to use another person's labor, and it will not benefit the company, in the long run. To provide the chance for employees to use their initiative and try out their own ideas is a form of experience. It makes their work more fulfilling, and it is also an important way to educate them. Managers should never forget that this is basic to the company that wants to grow.

Chapter Seven

The Ideal Manager

1. The Million-Dollar Knack

IN the early days of Matsushita Electric I used to address my staff every morning. It was a good way to practice my speech training, and also to let them know what I was thinking. In 1934, at our first meeting of the year, I said to them:

> As the new year begins, it gives me great pleasure to see our company making such healthy progress. It is entirely a result of intelligent, hard work. However, with the expansion of a company comes expansion of the responsibilities of management. As president of our company, it is I who set the guidelines; whether or not your efforts are utilized to the fullest will be a very good measure of my leadership. It is incumbent upon me to make sure your efforts are well spent. But I want you to rest assured that our company is run on sound policies and is going in the right direction.
>
> Nonetheless, I hope you will not stop just at doing well. Each of you is also your own manager. You should always keep your managerial goals in sight, fulfilling them through your work. You will gain wisdom and make new discoveries through the proper performance of your job, and what you learn, while helping you to grow as people, is what will support the growth of the company. There is a lot of truth in the adage, "The knack for successful management is worth a million dollars." If you really want to acquire that knack, you'll find that making so much money is not so difficult.

Some fifty years have passed since I made that speech, but I am more convinced than ever that wealth is within easy reach of those who have grasped the true knack of successful management. Its first hallmark is active business.

Take two coffee shops of equal size, both situated in a busy shopping center. In objective circumstances, the chances are even for either to succeed or to fail. However, if one of them is always busy while the other is usually half-empty, the difference lies in the managers. One has the knack of selling while the other does not. The same applies to any kind of business, whether it is a shop or a company.

How do you acquire this knack? There is, unfortunately, no tried and true technique. Unlike business administration, the essentials of which can be taught, a knack for something comes through experience and discovery of one's own innate skills. It is more like an awakening to the truth.

To some extent, it can be self-taught. One way to find and develop those skills is for the manager to reflect on his actions and decisions of each day to see which can be counted as successes and which as failures. If he perseveres in this exercise until it becomes automatic, he will find that he is making fewer and fewer mistakes of judgment. At that point he is well on his way to grasping the knack of successful business.

Also important is always to keep an open mind, unfettered by personal desires or prejudices and able to see things as they really are. That is harder than it sounds, since our education has molded our outlook, for the most part, and conditioned us to see things with only limited vision. Acquiring a knack for successful management is, therefore, time-consuming for well-educated people. Nevertheless, I find that open-mindedness—freedom from obsessions—is the single most important key to making sound judgments in daily life, and especially in business.

2. Food for Thought

NOT long after starting up my own business, I remember hearing a story that impressed me deeply at the time, and which I have never forgotten. To retell it briefly, one afternoon in the days when Japan was still far from affluent, a beggar came into a large, established confectioner's to buy a *manju* (Japanese bean jam-filled bun). The assistant, startled at seeing such a lowly customer in his first-class establishment, hastily wrapped the manju, but before he could hand it over to the beggar, the shop owner entered and called out, "Just a minute, let me wait on him." So saying, he gave the package to the beggar and, when he was paid, he bowed politely and said, "Thank you very much for your patronage."

Afterwards the boy asked the owner, "Why did you wait on him yourself? You have never done that before for any other customer. It is always me or the chief clerk who handles sales."

The owner replied, "I can understand why you are bewildered. But we should be pleased and grateful that this particular customer came in today, and I wanted to express my thanks. Naturally we value our regular customers, but this case was special."

"Why was it special?" the boy asked.

"Almost all our customers are well off, and for them it is routine to buy their confections here. But that man wanted one of our manju so badly that he may have spent everything he had on it. I knew it was very important to him, and so I decided that he should be served by the owner himself. That is what business is all about."

It is a simple, yet beautiful story. It made me realize that every customer is entitled to equal respect; a customer's worth is never dependent upon his personal prestige or the size of his purchase. I think this is where a real businessman finds joy, and this is where his values should lie.

3. Confidence with Humility

In whatever you do, act with confidence and faith. Those qualities are important in daily life, and perhaps even more so in business dealings or in managing a company. An enterprise without faith, or a business concern that lacks confidence, will not make much of a contribution to anyone. An enterprising and earnest manager, therefore, has to nurture principles that will steadily raise the confidence of his firm as a whole.

The sensitive aspect of trying to stick to given principles, no matter how important they are, is to gain support for them without forcing them on anyone. They must be based on humility. Confidence without humility is closer to arrogance. Think about some of the people you know who have failed in business. Not always, but often they lacked humility and were highly opinionated. In contrast, if confidence grows gradually in a humble person, it crystallizes into firm, positive principles, which in most cases will guide that person to achieve his goals.

People who have others working under them must be doubly careful about lining their confidence with humility. Whereas their subordinates can be cautioned when their attitudes or actions are not constructive, no one can point out errors of judgment or conduct to the men at the top. That is why they must constantly examine their attitudes for themselves.

People with humility are able to detect greatness in others, and as a consequence they can recognize when one of their subordinates is more skilled than they are. If you assume that your employees, because they are subordinate, are less skilled or talented than you, it is a sign that you lack humility. Certainly not all your employees are superior workers, but your own humility will let you appreciate their merits better and you will understand how to use them and their ideas well.

4. No Security Is Foolproof

SOME years ago there was a lot of talk of a "distribution revolution" in Japan. A barrage of new products were appearing on the market, and consumer tastes were changing rapidly, which paved the way for the inevitable, huge supermarket chains to spring up all over the country. These new enterprises had a profound effect on the system of distribution. They started a trend that has affected all businesses, creating a whole new set of worries and headaches in the process.

No one is immune, least of all manufacturers. We are all uneasy about a very uncertain future. Yet is this not the way it has always been? I do not think we can, or should, ever assume that absolute security is even possible in business. There is nothing new in our situation, and I am sure that no individual, in any era, has been free of worries regarding the future. We simply have to deal with our circumstances and find ways to resolve them.

Few achievements are made without great effort and anxiety. The pace and quality of change in society today are naturally disturbing, but is it not in drastic change that we find proof of our own existence, and, by extension, joy in living? Simply to bemoan our fate robs us of the stimulation of challenge, and it solves nothing. On the other hand, if we never had any worries, and never had to face hard work, we would stagnate and management methods would become flabby and prosaic.

Our world is not calm, but to keep a business going demands a firm determination to persevere. For the sake of our customers, we should be constantly updating our business methods to find the best means of responding to our changing world. If anywhere, perhaps, it is in such efforts themselves that security is to be found.

5. The General Decides

WHEN a single decision can affect the future of a company, the person charged with decision-making carries a heavy burden. Yet it is this responsibility that gives meaning to his career.

Is there any basic rule to follow in making decisions? Generally, to exercise common sense and caution largely assures a wise decision, but today, increasingly, that is not necessarily enough. More and more we are required to move quickly and boldly. Thus, a certain daring, as well as prudence, is necessary today, and the successful manager must know where the right balance lies in each case.

To make the right decision means being able to assess a situation accurately. Personal gain, fame, or wealth must never be factors in a decision. The wise decision, rather, depends on an open, unprejudiced outlook not hampered by preconceptions, a perspective that allows one to see the situation objectively and in terms of the larger goal.

Decisions are not made in a vacuum—many people influence each stage. And they are important; to consider the various points of view and opinions is valuable in preventing one from becoming too dogmatic. We should listen, and appreciate their merits, and at the same time recognize when well-meant suggestions are off the mark. Every manager can benefit enormously by learning his staff's ideas, reactions, and suggestions. But to use that feedback well, he must have refined powers of discernment.

The duty of a staff officer is to work out feasible strategies and present them to the general. Sometimes ten strategists can come up with a unified plan, but more often they will present several different ones. The general must study them, decide which is best, or how to combine the best ideas in all of them. If he cannot do that much, his strategy will falter and he will be routed.

In that sense, the company president is like a general. Only he can make the decisions for his employees to follow. His business will be successful only if he can provide the kind of leadership that capitalizes on the wisest options.

6. Final Responsibility

WHETHER a company prospers or fails is ultimately up to the president, the man in charge. It is true that social, political, or other factors can affect the company's performance, but the final responsibility rests with the president alone.

Take a staff problem, for example. Suppose some of your employees resist your directives; the first person to blame is yourself, because if you had given them proper guidance in the first place, including the motivation to work together, your employees would express their differences of opinion in a constructive way. If they continue to be antagonistic, there must be something wrong with your own ideals. Therefore, before you blame them, first critically examine yourself.

Again, when people are pushed into a tight corner, only their weak side comes out. They do not function well under those circumstances. If you have been too hasty in reproaching someone, for instance, or have assessed a situation incorrectly, whatever the circumstances, you owe it to those working for you to take the responsibility. If you are aware of your responsibility and carry it out, that attitude will be conveyed to your employees, and, with a sense of responsibility for themselves, they will not be put on the defensive. In an environment where all the staff are responsible for themselves, business will develop and prosper. Then you can see the maxim, "Work, and you will be rewarded," come to life.

In short, whether you run a small shop or manage a large company, each one of your employees should be conscious of his responsibility for himself. That attitude can take root only if the president is aware that the final responsibility is his.

7. A Lifetime Occupation

I talk constantly about how a good manager must have strong convictions, or a sense of mission in his work, but I know it is not easy to develop and sustain such qualities. In my own case, when I started my own business, I put everything I had into my work, just to keep afloat. Then as the years passed and the number of people in the company increased, I began to feel uneasy, disturbed that our operations were just routine, with no particular purpose. I became convinced that a corporate leader had to have some other raison d'être for his company. He needed an ideal, a sense of mission that would constantly encourage him and help him become better qualified to guide and inspire those under him.

Since that time, I have formed my own basic convictions about what our company should be, and I have worked with a sense of mission. It has made such a difference to me that I often talk about these things with my workers, hoping that they, too, will develop their own convictions. More than once I have been caught in an agonizing dilemma because of my ideals, and I have been tempted to compromise them. But each time, somehow I gathered the strength to stick to what I believe in, even though it meant some hard decisions. And each time, I grew more certain of my mission, surer of my beliefs.

It seems to me that the forcefully self-assertive person is actually not very certain of himself. He needs to develop faith in himself and in what he is doing, which can come about only by constantly criticizing and encouraging himself. If he works at that day by day, he will gain the steady assurance to remain firm in his convictions when he has to make important decisions. No matter what job a person does, to do it well means long training and the quest for self-improvement, and that is a lifetime occupation.

8. Umbrella in the Rain

Nearly twenty years ago, soon after I left the president's post at Matsushita Electric to become chairman of the board, a young news reporter gathering material for an article asked to see me. He opened with a curious question. "Mr. Matsushita," he said, "your company has grown so incredibly quickly; what, in your opinion, is the secret of such successful growth?"

For a moment I did not know what to say. If there was some "secret" to the way we had prospered, I could not think how to put it in a few words. Then I hit upon an idea. I asked the young reporter, "What would you do if you were caught in a rainstorm?" My apparently irrelevant question took him by surprise. He hesitated, trying to figure out what to answer. Finally he came up with the sensible reply, "I would take out an umbrella, of course."

"Right," I said. "When it rains, you put up an umbrella. That is the secret of success in business and management." The reporter looked even more puzzled than before.

It is only common sense to use an umbrella when it rains —otherwise one gets wet. It is a routine, natural response to a natural phenomenon. Any secret to successful growth in business and industry also consists in operating on a common sense basis, in a natural, unforced way. In sales, for example, it is only logical to set a price on a product that takes into account the time, place, and circumstances, and makes a profit. You must also collect the proceeds of your sales. If your products do not sell well, it is not logical to force sales by ignoring profit. Give them time; wait until they begin to sell again at your price. That is just as sensible as umbrella in the rain. If you follow this principle steadily without lapsing, it will automatically assure success in business and management.

Yet while we do not think twice about putting up an umbrella in the rain, the natural response seems a lot more difficult when it comes to business and management. As a result, many times people make the wrong decisions from misplaced judgment, because they let selfish motives take precedence over common sense. They soon find themselves out in the rain with no umbrella.

A great many entrepreneurs try to undercut competition by

selling their products below cost, and others borrow funds while the proceeds from what they have sold sit neglected, waiting to be claimed until the customers ask them to come and collect the money. Those are not practices that lead to success in business. To earn a profit, you must sell goods at a price that is higher than wholesale cost. Before borrowing money, the sensible businessman collects all outstanding bills. Only after receiving the proceeds due him does he borrow money, if, indeed, a loan is still necessary. That is the logical, common-sense way to operate. It is the way nature works. Abiding by such simple and ordinary practices faithfully and routinely is the key to success, not only in business, but in many other activities as well.

PART TWO

1. No Such Thing as Failure

You are about to make a decision that could change the whole direction of your life. How to approach it? Virtually everyone comes to such a critical juncture at least once. You cannot make that decision casually, for it affects many others around you. To plunge off in the wrong direction may cost them as dearly as it costs you. On the other hand, to let the fear of failure immobilize you will stop you from ever trying anything new, and yours will be the loss in personal growth and fuller human relations.

In June 1917, at the age of twenty-two, I resigned from the Osaka Electric Light Company (now Kansai Electric Power Company) where I had worked for seven years, to start my own business. To break with my company like that was, in 1917, equivalent to the move many young men make today to give up their salaried security in search of something more fulfilling, if risky. My action, too, was regarded as unconventional and sheer folly. But I had chosen a new path for myself, and I had three reasons for doing so: dissatisfaction with life as a company employee, something my father once said to me, and an invention—I had devised new kind of light socket.

There was certainly nothing wrong with my company or the way they treated me. In fact, I had been promoted from an ordinary installations worker to inspector, and for that position, my working conditions were actually very good. It may be that they were *too* good. I could complete my required duties in half a day, and structure the remaining half as I saw fit. Such an ideal situation might seem rare. Indeed—what more could I ask?

At first, I felt very lucky, but after a month or two as an

inspector, I grew restless and unsatisfied. I was young and energetic. I wanted something I could give myself to wholly, something whose very demands on me created fulfillment. To idle away half the day grew tedious, and then it rankled. It was a problem of goals and challenge. To be in an enviably easy position in the company was not enough for me. I wanted to be excited about my work, and to put everything I had into it.

The second reason I decided to resign was some advice my father had given me long before, when I was a young apprentice at a bicycle shop. Someone had suggested that I leave the bicycle shop and take a job as a junior clerk with the Osaka Postal Savings Bureau. My mother and I were both attracted to the idea, but my father was against it. "Get into business for yourself. That's going to be your best bet," he said to me. "If you succeed, then you can do the hiring and get really well qualified people to work for you. You won't get anywhere as a junior clerk." I never forgot that. There was no more talk of the Savings Bureau. I left the bicycle shop to start working at the Osaka Electric Light Company, a firm I had chosen myself. By the time I resigned, my father was no longer living, but I have thought many times since, how right he was.

Third, and this clinched it, was the fact that my new light socket was never even given a chance in the company. In the course of my work, which involved wiring, I had been experimenting with sockets, trying to come up with one that was more convenient, easy to use, and secure than the standard ones then in use. Finally I devised a new, improved socket.

One day I proudly presented my socket to my supervisor, thinking that the company might well consider using it. He rejected it outright. "We have absolutely no use for something like this," said he, dismissing it. I was thoroughly irritated. This man may be a supervisor, but he can't even distinguish between a good socket and a bad one, I thought, smarting under the rebuff. Later, I realized that my socket indeed had been far from perfect, but at the time I was so confident of its merits and wanted so badly to see it manufactured for general use that its rejection came as a deflating blow.

And so, fired by the need to produce something positive myself, I left an unusually good job with a prominent firm and started out on my own. Naturally, after seven years, I still felt a strong attachment to the company, and I was also somewhat uneasy about the future. Would I be able to make a go of it? But, despite my anxiety, I was a twenty-two-year-old full of youthful optimism, and my hope of success was stronger than my fear of failure. I was excited, heading into a new world and new experience. Moreover, in the chance—which I thought was very small—that I didn't make it independently, I could always go back to my old company and work there for life. That knowledge sustained me in my determination to keep going, once I had started. It also made me less fearful of an uncertain future, and it gave me the courage to start a new, independent life.

As it happened, there were many trying times ahead, but I did not have to go back to my old job. When my business began to grow, and whenever the risks seemed especially daunting, I kept in mind the knowledge that I could always pick up from where I had left off. Once I was asked what I would do if I failed. I replied immediately, "I'll set up a noodle shop. I'll make the best noodles in town and leave all my customers happy."

I believe there is really no such thing as failure. That is the conviction that gives us courage and confidence in life.

2. Vagaries of Fate

WE are only human, and often we simply cannot see our way out of certain problems. This is especially true for young people, who have little experience in decision-making.

Toward the end of 1919, a man I will call Ando, a colleague from my Osaka Electric days, suggested that we try a new venture together. "Why work so hard by yourself when you can be manager of a corporation? It can be started with borrowed funds. I have relatives and friends with money, and I can easily raise $25,000 to $50,000 quite quickly. Why don't we join forces and incorporate this small venture? It could become much bigger that way."

His very earnestness moved me, and I was beginning to think that it might be better to join up with him. Together, with hard work, we could achieve what thirty people could do, instead of continuing on my own, trying to do the work of ten people by myself. "Give me a few days to think it over. I'll come around to see you later," I replied.

I thought over his proposal carefully, but I couldn't decide what to do. I weighed all the pros and cons, but was unable to envision which would be better, to form a company or continue on my own. This indecision and anxiety continued for two or three days, and finally, nothing resolved, I set out to Mr. Ando's house. I was very depressed.

The first thing he asked was, "Have you made up your mind? If you are game, I'll resign tomorrow and go back to my hometown. I can collect $2,500 from each of ten relatives there. That will give us $25,000 straight away. What do you say?" He pushed me hard to make up my mind, and even tried to force me into a decision, but I had only one year of business experience and I lacked any sense of my own future.

In short, I was as naive and as helpless as a child. Eventually I gave in to Ando, although inwardly I was still doubtful about the whole thing.

When I got home, the more I thought about it, the more qualms I had. I had been too hasty and had been trapped into deciding to form a company with Ando without having given enough thought to his character, his ability, or even his reliability. Could he really raise such a large amount of cash so easily? His assurances began to seem too casual and impractical, and I began to be very dubious about the whole thing.

It did not take me long to conclude that it was better to continue on my own, even though I might never make more than a small and limited contribution to the world of business. I felt badly about having to break my word to Ando and for two or three days I did nothing about it. Finally, unable to put it off any longer, I went to see him again, this time feeling guilty as well as depressed.

When I arrived I was greeted by Ando's wife, who told me some astounding news. Apparently he had contracted acute pneumonia the day after my visit and had passed away two days later. Mrs. Ando apologized for not informing me of his funeral, but she hadn't been able to find my address. I was absolutely stunned. Fate, with its unpredictable hand, had cancelled my promise in a single flourish. Had that promise been kept, Matsushita Electric would not exist today.

It took me some time to digest it all, but I could see at last the truth in the warning never to make a decision in haste, risking a bad mistake. Yet decisions should not be made too slowly either, risking loss of a valuable opportunity. Finally, you should never make decisions when only partly convinced. Not until you have considered all possible points and are fully convinced should you make a final decision.

3. All or Nothing on a Bicycle Lamp

NO business is carried on without certain risks. In some cases they are fatal; the company comes to a dead end and goes bankrupt. For that reason, I think it is generally wise to avoid risks as much as possible. But occasions do arise when a risk is justified, indeed, demanded by the circumstances.

In March 1923, Matsushita Electric started manufacturing battery-powered bicycle lamps. There were three types of bicycle lamps in use then: candle lamp, acetylene gas lamps, and another type of battery-powered lamps. All three had certain problems. The candle lamps were extinguished too easily by the wind, and one had to keep getting off to relight them. It was very irritating, as I myself remember all too well. The gas lights were complicated to handle, and expensive. And the battery-powered lamps, which had just come on the market, were still primitive, with a short life of only two or three hours.

I started to think about how the battery-powered lamps could be improved, this being a suitable project for my line of work. I experimented and produced several models, but none was what I wanted. About six months and a hundred or so more models later, at last I came up with the right one. The new model was a shell-type battery lamp enclosed in a wooden casing. I was sure it would have wide appeal because it had a life of thirty to fifty hours—more than ten times that of any other lamp on the market. It represented a huge improvement and an epoch-making new product. Best of all, it could be priced lower even than the candle lamps. It seemed to me that it would sell very well, and I decided on a large-scale production schedule.

Just as soon as I organized our sales campaign, however, I

discovered that we were up against a completely unexpected barrier. Our potential customers were simply not prepared for our long-life lamp. Convinced that no battery could last more than two or three hours, they gave us no credibility at all. Distributors and shopkeepers alike reacted the same way. When I tried to explain that our lamps were completely different from the old two- or three-hour ones, and much better, they shook their heads, saying, "Afraid not, thank you. Battery lamps just aren't going to sell. Better take them back with you."

I was dumbfounded and quite disturbed. How ironic that my lamps, which I knew were superior and which I had thought users would welcome, should be rejected out of hand. How dense they all were, I thought. Then I calmed down and began to see that I had not done enough to let buyers discover for themselves just how good my lamps really were. Obviously, words alone would not do the trick. People would change their minds only if they could see how exceptional my lamps were with their own eyes. But I had to move fast. The factory was turning them out rapidly and bicycle lamps were piling up in all our warehouses. I had to reach a large number of customers and I didn't have a moment to lose.

Finally I hit upon a plan that I thought would work. I would hire several people to go around to all the bicycle shops with my lamps. We would turn them on and display them prominently at the shops, leaving them burning for as long as the batteries lasted. That way, both distributors and customers could not but notice how strong my long-life lamps were.

We were taking a big risk, because the displays were free—no sales were involved. Because the shops were not under any obligation to buy, there was no guarantee that I would ever get any return on them. For a small firm to distribute free samples so widely was a big gamble; if the lamps did not sell it would mean that both my product and my management policy had failed. On top of that I would lose my investment—and that would be the end of my business.

It was a big challenge, and I took it with some trepidation, but it was the only card I had to play. Also, I was convinced of the competitive quality of my product. Once I made buyers aware of its superiority, I was sure that sales would be very good. I recalled the proverb, "Nothing ventured, nothing gained." If a person avoids all risks, he will never achieve much, but if he can disregard security at certain crucial times to rise to the challenge, a new road will open up. So I took the risk.

This story had a happy ending. My gamble paid off, and shops, having seen that my lamps really withstood the test of thirty to forty hours' continuous burning, started recommending them to their customers. The orders poured in. Distributors also placed orders and the lamps became a popular favorite nationwide. For me, this experience confirmed the truth of that old proverb, which, even now, acts to refuel my courage whenever I am faced with a difficult decision.

4. Better Safe than Bankrupt

GREED is one part of human nature, and in business when there is profit to be made, everyone tries to get a hand in. The immediate jostling for a share is to be expected, but if it turns into cutthroat competition, those who lose out lose everything in failure and bankruptcy. We see so much of this kind of bitter competition these days that it almost seems normal. But it is neither necessary nor beneficial for anyone. We should not allow excessive competition to put a man out of business.

Around 1925, on a trip to our branch office in Tokyo, I saw some of the new radio tubes that had just come on the market. That display was my first glimpse of radio tubes. Our branch manager told me that sales were slowly picking up in Tokyo and perhaps I should try marketing them in Osaka. I was intrigued by the vacuum tubes, and thought they might sell. I asked him to negotiate our purchase with the manufacturer.

The manufacturer ran only a small plant, however, and he said his factories could not handle the extra volume we were asking for. I decided to pay him in advance for 1,000 units, on the condition he supply as many as he could to Osaka.

Our Osaka wholesalers were enthusiastic about handling the radio tubes, which were still a novelty then, and the demand far exceeded the supply. In the end, Matsushita Electric made a handsome profit in only five or six months.

Then other manufacturers began to have the same idea, and within a short time the market was glutted with radio tubes, the price falling all the time. At this rate, I realized, our profit margin would soon be very thin. Our windfall had disappeared.

How does one cope with change of this sort? I believed that one should not look to the present but to the future in deciding how to react. I cancelled all our dealing in vacuum tubes, which was too bad, in a way, because they were very popular. But the changing situation was clear, and, on the most pragmatic level, we had already made a very good profit on what had been, in fact, a chance venture.

I informed our manufacturer and wholesalers. The manufacturer was only too pleased because he could now supply directly to the wholesalers, who also had no objections. Four or five months later, the price of radio tubes, already down, suddenly dropped sharply, and the companies involved in them were in serious financial trouble.

This simple event brought home to me the importance of timing, combined with moderation, in what we do. It was also a concrete example of the pitfalls of excessive competition. Obsessive profit-seeking makes us vulnerable to overcompetition, which ultimately damages all sides.

5. Demand Forecast as a Well-Hedged Bet

ALL of us in manufacturing aim at producing high-quality goods and selling them at low prices, although, more often than not, we fall short of our goal. Quality adds to cost, which inevitably pushes the price up; keeping prices low will mean either sacrificing quality or, maintaining quality, mass production and sales. The snag is that it is often hard to predict whether a certain product will generate mass sales or not.

My company added an electrothermal department in January 1927 to handle the manufacture of electric irons. At the time, the total demand for irons in Japan stood at less than 100,000 units per year. Their prices were so high that irons were beyond the reach of most housewives.

The whole raison d'être of the new department was to turn out solid, reliable irons and price them so that many more families could benefit by this useful item in daily life. To manufacture them as cheaply as possible would be self-defeating, since housewives disappointed with their poor quality would be back where they started—lacking a good, reasonably priced iron. Our irons had to be of comparable, and preferably better quality than those available on the market, and 30 percent cheaper.

As we discussed the various aspects of production, we found that the crucial factor was quantity. Given the fact that the total demand for irons then stood at about 8,000 units per month, could we produce 10,000 irons a month, in a new design, and expect to sell them? In addition to the models already on the market, could Matsushita Electric hope to sell that many more units per month? Common sense told us that we were looking at a virtually impossible goal; the market was not going to double overnight. The whole venture was extremely risky. Yet to manufacture a smaller number would cancel out economies of scale. We would have to keep our prices up, and fewer households would be able to own one, which would defeat the original purpose. The price had to come down by a large 30 percent margin.

Our engineering staff worked arduously to come up with a new design, and in four months our electric iron appeared on the market, retailing at 30 percent less than other irons. The result was overwhelming. Customers were delighted with both the quality and the price, and we not only met, but increased, our original target of 10,000 units per month. The problem that had given us such nightmares at the start resolved itself when customers discovered the new product.

If the price is right, a good product will sell—I began to see this as a truism. The deciding factor is how convinced one is in the first place of the product's saleability and usefulness. I was convinced, because I could foresee a large potential market demand. I could have assumed that there would be no demand for irons because current sales stood below 10,000 units per month. But instead, I predicted that if their prohibitive prices were lowered, demand would grow considerably.

I still do not claim to know how to forecast demand, but one thing I do know is that all human beings want to improve their standard of living. And if we can produce goods at a price within the reach of most people, demand for them will rise as predictably as human desire for the product.

People differ, of course, but if the desire for improvement is a basic instinct common to us all, demand, as well as new products, will know no limits. This is an attitude—or conviction—that supports positive and progressive decisions concerning products a manufacturer believes will benefit society and make daily life more comfortable.

6. Ill-Fated Partnership

EVERYONE makes mistakes from time to time. That is a truism of human nature. What is important, however, is not the mistake, but what we do about it. We can deny our failure, or pretend to ignore it, but a negative, defensive attitude does nothing to help us become a mature, responsible person.

Once we make a mistake, we must first admit it, then reflect on why it happened to begin with, and, depending on the reasons for it, try to correct or make up for it. That is a difficult process, but it helps us avoid repeating the mistake, and it is a way to let us grow as people.

I recall a humbling experience shortly after we set up our electrothermal department in 1927. Its first product was an electric iron, the Super Iron, as it was called. Its high quality and reasonable price made it very popular. In fact, in 1930, it was nominated a "Superior Quality Home Appliance" by the Ministry of Commerce and Industry.

Yet, strangely enough, the new department was not making money. I wondered what was wrong. Were our planning and marketing policies off the mark? I looked carefully into the operation of the new department and came to the conclusion that the problem lay in the management of the department itself.

Officially, the electrothermal department was under Matsushita Electric's management, but in fact, it was jointly managed by my friend and partner, Mr. Takeyama (pseudonym), and one of the Matsushita Electric engineers. I simply checked up from time to time. Takeyama owned a rice shop and had no previous experience in electric appliances. He was managing his shop while also being responsible for the electrothermal department. Thus, both Takeyama and I were giving the new project only half our attention, and that was the root of the trouble.

As the reason for the department's phlegmatic performance became clearer, I saw that I had to discontinue the partnership and put all my energy into the new project myself. But it was difficult to ask a friend to resign, especially as he had done as well as he could. Yet that was the only way to save the department. Takeyama was not to blame for any of this; it was my mistake and I had to remedy it.

I informed Takeyama immediately of what I had decided to do. "It was my mistake to put you in charge without helping you as much as I could," I said. "If I had paid more attention to the new department, you could have managed it with no trouble. I take the blame for its poor performance. Now I'm going to concentrate on it and let you give more time to your own business."

Takeyama was reluctant to leave, however, and so I proposed that he become an employee of Matsushita Electric. I was pleased that he accepted. The electrothermal department recovered, and we added new items—electric heaters and *kotatsu* (electric footwarmers) among them—to the product line, building a base for further growth.

Errors should be corrected as soon as we can admit them. It is not always easy, but we must realize that we are responsible for our own mistakes.

7. Clear the Warehouses!

It is not always easy to stick to what is essentially right in a given endeavor. Choices that ordinarily are clear can become muddled when long-held assumptions confront new situations. It is important to constantly examine the direction we are taking to make certain it is the right one.

Toward the end of 1929, business was so bad that Matsushita Electric was cornered into considering a drastic move that might have deeply harmed the company and a great many people. A crisis had arisen, and my top management could see no way out except to cut our workforce by half. Such a move went completely against the grain of our most basic principles and sense of fairness.

The crisis had been triggered by the announcement that the gold embargo was about to be lifted in Japan. The market suddenly shrank, sales plummeted, and countless factories were forced to shut down. There was a run on banks that left bankruptcies scattered in its wake. All over the country companies were cutting back on wages and laying off workers. Labor disputes erupted around the nation.

And, the warehouses of Matsushita Electric filled up with unsold stock as sales sagged, falling to less than half the usual volume. By the end of December 1929, less than a month after the announcement, we had no more warehouse space. With more funds, we could have maneuvered, but as things stood, it was clear that we would go under if something was not done.

To complicate matters, I happened to be in bed with a pulmonary ailment when my top staff came to discuss what they proposed to do about pulling the company out of its precarious situation. Briefly, they wanted to halve production by halving the workforce. In theory, their solution was sensible, and had I been the usual type of manager, I would have supported it. But before I approved any action, I wanted to think about what such a dire move meant. Would it be consistent with the "right" course our company was committed to? Clearly we were in serious difficulty, but was the only remedy to place half our workforce in the ranks of the unemployed?

The future of the company lay in expansion; to discharge even one employee whom I had the good fortune to hire ground against company policy, and my own instincts as well. There had to be an alternative that did not require such a huge sacrifice.

Actually, there were two specific problems we had to solve. One concerned production—in no way could we maintain our current level and remain in business—but how to cut production without cutting the workforce? The answer to that was to cut production to half by working only half a day, but work the half-day at full force. That would mean an additional loss, but it would be only temporary. The other problem was to find a way to sell our surplus stock quickly, as the goods were not meant to be stored for long periods. We would have to put all our energy into this one.

Our executives came up with several proposals and ideas, which I considered carefully, and then I announced a solution that was unorthodox but worth a try. "We will cut production by half, as of today," I told them, "but no one will be fired. We will work half days but everyone will be paid full-time wages. In return, I will ask every employee in the company to devote all his free time, including Sundays and holidays, to selling our surplus stock and clearing the warehouses."

They welcomed this idea with enthusiasm. When we

informed our factory workers of the decision, they were vastly relieved, overjoyed, in fact. Much encouraged by this unusual approach to a serious situation, all of them cooperated fully, and two months later the warehouses were empty. Not too long after that our factories were able to resume the normal full-day production schedule, but even that soon became inadequate to handle the rising volume of orders.

It is logical enough to assume that if sales are down to half, then production, and consequently manpower, must also be halved. But the formula is not very humane. It is not right because it sacrifices people—the heart of a company. When its products are not selling, a company must put all its resources into sales until the slump is over. It must not compromise its integrity as employer or producer in favor of short-range solutions that could cause permanent damage.

8. The Customer Comes First

DETERMINATION is one thing, but stubborn persistence in a narrowly conceived point of view is another. To stick to your position and ignore the perspectives of others can be damaging, but unfortunately it happens all too often. If the conflict between your own determination and the interests of others grows too intense, you lose your sense of balance and then things begin to go wrong. It is very important to consider the interests of other people, but that is easier said than done.

In 1930, Matsushita Electric started selling radios, which were gaining popularity in Japan. Radios in those days were plagued with all kinds of faults, and nothing irritated me more than having my favorite programs interrupted because of malfunctions. There was enough complaining that our distributors urged us to start manufacturing radios ourselves.

Convinced that high-quality radios were a social necessity, I was eager to enter the business, but there was one problem: we had absolutely no experience in radio production. The alternative was to ask another company to make radios that we would sell under our brand. A long search turned up K Factory, which seemed very well suited to our purposes, and we signed a contract for the production of radios.

The results were devastating. A stream of defective sets began coming back to us until they were piled high in our warehouses. Our distributors were alarmed and I was shocked. And I had had such confidence in the work of K Factory!

It was useless to rant and rave, however, and so I started digging into the reasons for the problems. It turned out that the troubles were minor and stemmed from sloppy work —loose screws or badly fitted tubes, things that could be fixed easily. But why were there so many returns? It so happened that our distributors were not experienced in handling radios and did not understand how they worked. K Factory previously had distributed its radios through dealers with some knowledge of the product. Every radio sent from the factory had been opened and inspected and, where necessary, had been repaired. They had arranged a good system that guaranteed very few returned radios.

Our sales network was mainly in the electric wiring field and the salesmen had no knowledge of radios, with the result that whatever was supplied by our factory was sold direct to the customer and returned if found faulty. Clearly, then, we should not use our regular sales channels for the distribution of radios.

But what to do? If we could not depend on our own sales outlets to provide fault-free radios to the customers, we could use K Factory's experienced dealers, who could check the radios first. But it was our distributors who had pressed us to manufacture radios in the first place. In all fairness, we could not simply abandon our own people, who had worked with us for so long, and switch to K Factory's dealers.

The only solution was to manufacture radios that had no faults and required no repairs, so our distributors could handle them. We should improve our product to satisfy our customers, not ask the customer to accept whatever we offered. We should place priority on our customers, making this the principle of our business.

And so I asked K Factory to manufacture radio sets that needed no repairs. When that proved impossible, we terminated our arrangement with the factory. Now we had no partner. We were back to square one. We could not give up the radio business, because we were already committed, and so I resolved that we would do everything ourselves. I instructed our research and development department to design a good, solid radio that functioned well. The research staff, having had no experience in radio design, were overwhelmed. Our chief engineer, Tetsujiro Nakao, sputtered, "We cannot possibly do this. Even if we can, it will take time."

I agreed, but I couldn't turn back or keep our customers waiting too long. We had also procured all of the necessary equipment, which was standing idle. I told Nakao, "We're cornered, and there is no time to waste. We may not have the necessary experience, but amateurs all over the country are assembling their own sets from parts sold on the market. Surely, with a proper laboratory and good equipment, you can do better than they. Why not give it a try. Sometimes when things have to be done in a short time, a person gets a flash of inspiration. If you really try, I'm sure you will succeed."

Nakao thought a bit, then he replied. "All right, let us try." They began work almost immediately. They were at it day and night for three months, and in that time they produced a fine model that performed very well. It so happened that NHK (Japan Broadcasting Corporation) was holding a radio contest and, for the experience, we entered our new model. Imagine our surprise when we were awarded first prize!

The episode taught me that whenever we are cornered, we should not waste time hemming and hawing about priorities, but plunge in immediately to find a solution, guided by the first principle: the customer comes first. That is what we did when we began to manufacture National radios, and they are still popular today.

9. Growth in Striving for a Goal

To lack goals is to be deprived of meaning and stimulation in life. To have a goal is to have a referent in day-to-day living, and it defines our responsibilities and purposes. It is the incentive to achieve something that makes each day worth tackling with vigor and enjoyment. How do we determine what is our overall mission in life? In my experience, I have found that not many people can envision their life purposes very clearly.

I found my own mission in life in 1932, after a visit to a temple community. A friend and customer, trying to convert me to a certain religion, had taken me to the main temple of his religion to observe the activities there as well as the fine buildings. Indeed, they gleamed proudly, not a speck of dust in sight, and I remember being impressed at seeing a group of believers praying by an altar.

I was even more impressed when I learned that the temple buildings had been built by the followers themselves. We visited a school, a library, and a sawmill where the timber for the buildings was cut, and we observed people quietly and diligently working on wood-processing activities. The atmosphere there was entirely different from the wood factory in town; somehow it inspired reverence.

Riding home on the train, and later, I mused about what I had seen. Businesses are often immobilized by recessions, yet this religion seemed so steady and prosperous. What was the difference? Was it that religious activities, bringing spiritual peace and enlightenment to people, are respected and can flourish on that support? Manufacturers do not serve the spirit. We supply goods that are necessary for living. A religion and a company serve people in different ways, but both are important.

Still, the fact remains, I thought, that religious activities seem so steady, while manufacturers keep going in and out of bankruptcy. Perhaps it is because religions concentrate on saving people, while industrialists are only interested in money. Was that the reason for the difference? Yet, I reasoned, manufacturers do not produce to satisfy their own needs, but the material needs of society. In this respect, we, too, perform a task of equal dignity. It is not just work, but work that will help people live, and for that reason it is a task beyond measurement. Our duty is to work hard to fulfill our responsibility well.

The more I thought, the more excited I became. I had discovered my purpose in life. At that juncture I became determined to pursue it positively. I realized then that Matsushita Electric's mission lies in manufacturing commodities that contribute to a better life, commodities in such abundance and so reasonable that no one can say he cannot afford them. There is a saying, "Poverty is more wretched than all the diseases the flesh is heir to." To remove material poverty is like alleviating pain, thereby giving solace to the human spirit. That was the process by which I found my own mission in life as a businessman, and that mission has continued to guide the way we run our business.

I wanted to convey my new-found understanding to our staff, and communicate to them the importance of making a united effort toward this goal. On May 5, 1932, I gathered all the staff together to tell them what had happened to me, that my whole outlook had crystallized into a clear objective. To commemorate the occasion, I declared it the founding day of Matsushita Electric and had a special ceremony performed. After my speech, many of the staff came up to the podium to offer their enthusiastic support. The whole hall seemed to vibrate with a new eagerness. Matsushita Electric at last had found its mission to society.

10. The Devil's Gate

ONE thing that seems to hold endless interest for people is the behavior of others. And often the observer simply cannot restrain himself from making certain that his opinion—praise or criticism—is known, especially when some action is unusually conspicuous. Whether you call it moralizing, preaching, gossip, when such judgments are critical, they can undermine one's confidence and cause his determination to teeter.

I found out exactly how harmful such thoughtless criticism can be when we moved our company to Kadoma, in the suburbs of Osaka, in 1933. The move attracted a lot of attention. It was not simply a matter of setting up another office; we were relocating the entire head office, and in addition, were planning to build several new factories in the area to accommodate the steadily increasing demand for our products. Finding no suitable site in Osaka, we decided on Kadoma, where we had already bought land to build employee training facilities.

However, when the move was announced, we were widely criticized, mainly on grounds of bad judgment in timing. It was too soon after the depression, it was claimed, to expand on such a large scale; it was "indiscreet" to expand so "ostentatiously" when so many other firms were barely managing to stay afloat. And we were warned that Kadoma, situated to the northeast of Osaka, was an unlucky location. The belief that the northeast, or "Devil's Gate," was unlucky, was passed down from ancient Chinese lore and geomancy, according to which all misfortune and suffering come from that direction. Actually, I myself was not completely immune to those superstitions. The selection of a new site was considered critically important to the success of the operation, and I did not want any interference from the direction of a "Devil's Gate," even in the form of public protest that we had chosen a bad site.

I was uneasy, to be sure, but we had not been able to find a suitable site in Osaka, and the Kadoma tract was really perfect for the new factories and offices. Its size alone assured room for further growth in the future. Even if Kadoma was considered an inauspicious location, I was not ready to pass it up and search for another, giving in to superstitious folklore.

Then it occurred to me that if the northeast direction is unlucky, then the whole of Japan, its innumerable islands laid out in a northeast-southwest arc, must also be unlucky. If we took the Devil's Gate prohibition seriously, we would have to move out of Japan altogether. Moving northeast to Kadoma might be an unlucky direction, but if we could ignore it, all would be well. With that rationalization, I breathed a sigh of relief and my last lingering doubts about the move vanished.

As for the accusations that we were being profligate and possibly reckless, in large part they stemmed from the fact that our methods of obtaining capital were not yet considered standard practice, and we relied on them at a time when other businesses were floundering for lack of capital. In short, we borrowed extensively from banks. Without bank loans, we could never have made the move and expanded at that time. But borrowing from banks was regarded then as an extremely unsound business practice, and I knew I would have to justify it to our critics. We were very fortunate in that our banks had confidence in us and lent us the necessary funds without the usual collateral.

I understood the opprobrium we had incurred on this score, and I tried to explain our position and dispel doubts in the formal announcement we printed when the new facilities were inaugurated.

> "...Our company is still young, but we are making every effort to carry out our many projects fully and well. At present, our commitments far exceed the resources we have to fulfill them, and we are, indeed, relying on outside funds. But our viability as a company is strong enough to absorb our debts and continue to grow."

This was directed at the rumors whispered behind our backs regarding our potential solvency. I suppose it was like a man acknowledging his crimes when humility is demanded to palliate the judges. People were implying that Matsushita Electric was indiscreet and arrogant, and I admitted as much in the announcement, which I thought was necessary to answer public criticism.

Still, the main reason I could parry the critics' thrusts with confidence was the solid, steady management of my company, which gave me enough support that I could be honest with the public. Later, several guests at the inauguration ceremony confided that my statement had been suprising, but impressive. Today, Kadoma is still the site of the corporate headquarters of Matsushita Electric, as well as the center of its research and development. I do not give any more credit to my foresight than I do to luck, but with hindsight, how deeply glad I am that I stuck to my original decision, in spite of criticism and some resentment from the public.

11. Divide and Succeed

If instructions are careful, all you need is memory to follow them. Thinking or initiative is not necessary. It might be very easy to live always by someone else's directions, but it would also be tedious and ultimately thwarting, because if you cannot use your own creativity, it is hard to muster interest or enthusiasm. That is why managers should keep in mind the importance of delegating responsibility to their subordinates. Given responsibility, the motivated employee will respond by doing his best, which will support the company's objectives and give the man himself valuable experience.

By 1933, it had become increasingly difficult to maintain adequate control over company operations under the existing management structure. We had celebrated our official inauguration the previous year, and the company was expanding steadily, guided by a clear vision of its responsibilities. We had more work, and new product lines; the sales and planning departments had grown larger; and new factories and sales offices were in the planning stage. To handle all the operations such growth required, Matsushita Electric adopted a new management structure that allowed me to delegate a lot of work to my staff.

Actually the company was still small enough that I could have managed it alone by supervising the work of each departmental manager. Had I been perfectly healthy, there would have been no real need to create our new system of divisions, but my health was not good at that time, and I could not attend all the necessary meetings with the departmental managers. Of course, they could have run their departments independently, but increasing business meant more functions and more problems, and it was more important than ever for me to meet with the managers regularly. But I was of little help on account of my illness. The efficiency of the whole company was being eroded and something had to be done. I could see that the managers would have to work without me for a while and make decisions by themselves. I could help in urgent cases, but that would certainly not be every day.

The situation meant that each of our managers would have to function autonomously, like the head of an independent company. I decided to partition the entire company and place a director in charge of each division. Former department heads would become division directors, with full and independent responsibility for the management of each. Whereas the former sales manager had handled only sales of manufactured products, the director of each new division would assume responsibility for planning all sales programs, production of new commodities, and even accounting. Indeed, each division would operate like a separate company.

The system went into effect in May 1933. Radios became the responsibility of the First Division; the Second Division handled batteries and lights; and wiring implements, synthetic resins, and electric heating appliances were the Third Division's responsibility. Because the new directors of each division worked with such enthusiasm, their spirit caught on among their subordinates, and the restructured system worked even better than expected. The directors worked hard and with imagination to make each division grow, and as a result, their activities multiplied. The business as a whole prospered under their leadership.

12. Toward Spiritual Affluence

PEOPLE can think and act in many different ways, and develop many different attitudes. They have constructive thoughts and do positive acts, and sometimes they think and act in a damaging or passive way. At times it is almost impossible to understand why someone acts the way he does. One can agonize over certain behavior, and still not know what to do about it. This is true, whether you are talking about individuals, groups, or society as a whole. It is easy enough to shrug it off, thinking you are powerless to help, but in some cases, something *can* be done.

At the end of World War II, Matsushita Electric was using all the raw materials it had in stock to keep home appliance production going, in an effort to help resuscitate the ailing Japanese economy. Very soon its stocks ran out, however, and because of the government's indefinite stance on iron and steel production, new raw materials supplies were not coming in. Even if new supplies had been available, there was no way to transport them and no fuel.

The economic situation was grim. So much had been destroyed during the war that a great many people seemed to have given up; they had no motivation to work. Our company was suffering, too, but I was responsible for the livelihood of tens of thousands of workers in my factories. There was no way whatsoever that I could give up.

Perhaps one individual can do very little when the problem is nationwide economic disaster and the collapse of morale, but I had to try. I could see that while Japan desperately needed to revive industry, nobody was motivated to the hard work necessary to get the factories going again. There was something very wrong. Perhaps, I thought, the depressing social and economic environment has discouraged everyone so much that they cannot see—or do not care about—what they must do. I wanted desperately to try to change that attitude.

I found myself wondering why, even though all people desire peace and happiness, we are so easily drawn into war and conflict with our fellow men. Is violence the real nature of man? Birds fill their stomachs and fly about enjoying life. Man, the supreme being, wages wars, suffers from hunger and dies of starvation. He should be able to create kinder conditions for himself.

Basically, the problem is within man himself. War and the disaster it brings are not natural phenomena—they are man's creation. Thus, if we want to eliminate misery from human life, we must first comprehend man. From such thoughts emerged the germ of the PHP (Peace and Happiness through Prosperity) idea. My friends urged me to use the idea as the basis of a group, a movement, dedicated to the same ideals. But as a businessman, a manufacturer of electric appliances, I wondered if I had enough educational background or knowledge to make it work. In any case, I did not want to waste time debating that. It had become an irresistible compulsion that drove me into initiating the movement.

On November 3, 1946, PHP Institute was founded. I drew on the wisdom of experts and studied the various ways to achieve prosperity, and in the process probed hard to learn the best ways to develop a truly peaceful, happy, and prosperous society.

The early years were by no means smooth, but as more and more people began to understand and rally behind the movement, PHP Institute expanded rapidly. Today, its wide range of activities includes the monthly magazine *PHP* (over one million circulation), English and Spanish language periodicals, and the journal *Voice,* as well as a large number of books. The institute also sponsors PHP Friendship Association meetings, PHP seminars, and many other endeavors aimed at actively promoting the ideals of Peace and Happiness through Prosperity.

13. Two Wheels in the Balance

It is generally assumed that a union works against the interests of management. I maintain, however, that a union can enhance a company's vitality and thus work in management's favor. The Matsushita Labor Union was formed in January 1946. Management in Japan did not like the idea of unions, especially in the immediate postwar period, when the democratic reforms gave rise to a rash of unions that appeared all over the country. Most industries that had unions found that their work was hampered by union demands. At the very least, management lost its exclusive decision-making power.

Since most company presidents did not attend the inaugural ceremonies of their union, my presence at the Matsushita Labor Union's inauguration surprised people. I had wanted to be there, because I felt a strong bond between my employees and me, and I thought the feeling was reciprocated. Now that my employees had established their own union, I naturally wanted to congratulate them.

The ceremony was held at the Nakanoshima Auditorium in Osaka. When I arrived, on January 30, the auditorium was already filled with some 4,000 members. At an appropriate time, I mentioned that I would like to express my congratulations. Instead of being rushed to the podium, I was asked to wait while the union leaders conferred. Then the chairman of the meeting addressed the gathering, saying, "Mr. Matsushita is in the audience and he wishes to speak. Shall we permit him to do so?" I was shocked. This was a whole new attitude—my employees seemed to have changed overnight. In any case, they allowed me to speak, and in my three-minute address I said:

> We are in a crucial period trying to reconstruct our nation after the terrible destruction of the war. The founding of your union is an important step toward the creation of a new Japan, one based firmly in the principles of democracy. I extend to you my heartfelt congratulations.
>
> Basically, I support unions. Through your union you will be able to decide many matters yourselves and present suggestions and requests to management. I heartily welcome all suggestions and demands that will benefit our nation and its citizens, including union members. But I will not listen to those that do not, and I will not approve them. On that basis, I want to join hands and proceed with the task of rebuilding our country.

There was thunderous applause when I finished speaking. The union members seemed to have sensed that I was absolutely sincere in telling them I would consider their suggestions and demands, unless they were too self-serving. That night I talked to Kanju Kato, the Japan Socialist party leader, who had been present at the ceremony. He told me that he had visited many companies throughout the country to push unionization and had been present at numerous inaugural meetings, but he had never found any top management representatives in attendance. "At Matsushita Electric," he continued, "I thought it was remarkable that the president himself was there to express his support of the union and to congratulate its members." I was happy that I had had the chance to forge the first link with our new union.

My attitude has remained the same toward unions and their activities. Indeed, the healthy growth of the Matsushita Labor Union is the strength of Matsushita Electric. Management must make efforts to shape a company that can accommodate and benefit from a growing union. To me, the union and the management are the two wheels of a wagon that hold up the company. If one wheel expands more than the other, the wagon will tilt. Only when both wheels are balanced can we move forward smoothly, together.

14. Pricetag on the Intangible

It is much more difficult to assign a value to a hidden, intangible asset than it is to a clearly defined, visible object, but it can be just as important. In business, managerial ability cannot be seen, but clearly it is worth a great deal more when it is strong than when it is weak, when it fosters growth in the company and higher standards of employee welfare. Superior management ultimately works to benefit society as a whole, which gives it a very high value indeed. Yet often this important asset is not correctly assessed.

In October 1952 Matsushita Electric entered into a technical cooperation agreement with the Dutch company N. V. Philips Gloeilampenfabrieken, and in December that year we set up an affiliated company, Matsushita Electronics Corporation. These events culminated long search in the United States and Europe to find the most suitable partner in our new venture. I considered several companies in the United States, all of which were strong and technically very advanced, but in scale and other ways as well, too different from us to make a feasible partnership, I thought. Then I went to the Netherlands. Like Japan, it is a small country, and N. V. Philips Gloeilampenfabrieken had been founded over sixty years before on the initiative of a single entrepreneur, and was still growing along the lines envisioned by its founder. Matsushita Electric and Philips seemed to have a lot in common, and I decided that this was the right partner. Soon thereafter I began negotiations for a technical cooperation agreement.

In the course of our discussions, a serious problem emerged concerning royalties. Philips asked for considerably more than the percent usually demanded by other firms. Philips justified its high rate by arguing that any company entering into a joint venture with Philips was assured of success, eminent success, in fact, which could not be said of most other joint ventures. Their supporting data showed records of factories in forty-eight countries, all of them doing extremely well.

As I listened to their case, I was impressed by their self-confidence and, mentally, I began to concede the high royalty rate. But not completely. The proposed percentage was still inordinately high. The simple solution would have been to call off negotiations and go to an American firm, but I could not shake off my sense that Philips was the right partner for us. The only obstacle lay in the sticky problem of royalties. I began to think about how to resolve it.

It seemed to me that there was probably little difference between Philips's technology and that of other firms. The main difference was that Philips was confident enough to take on the responsibility of ensuring success. In other words, Philips was charging for technology as well as its application.

Then I began to see a way to make it work. If my reasoning was correct, then the abilities of those who pay the royalties should also be called into play. Just as there are good teachers and bad, so are there exceptional students and mediocre ones. Philips was asking for a higher royalty because its management considered the company a good teacher, but in Matsushita Electric's case, they had failed to consider the ability of the student.

At our next meeting, I informed them that, "If you enter into a technical cooperation agreement with Matsushita, I give you my word that the results will be better than with any other firm you have dealt with so far. If your average level of success is 100, with Matsushita, it will be 300. Now, the management expertise that we will provide to our joint venture also has a price. Under the circumstances, I propose that we pay you a royalty for technical know-how, while you pay Matsushita Electric a royalty for management expertise."

They were stunned. "Such a fee is unheard of," they argued, but I elaborated. I explained that if our management produced results worth more than the fee, they would lose nothing, whereas their 30 percent share could be wiped out if the joint venture were not managed properly. Wouldn't that consideration alone make the fee worth paying, I asked them. I assured them that I was completely confident about our management. "You supply the technology and we pay for it," I said, "but it is up to our management to make that investment pay off." In the end, they gave in. We concluded the technical cooperation agreement exactly as I had proposed.

I was pleased that we had been able to strike what seemed to me a fair bargain, for I really believed that technical collaboration should take into account the managerial aptitude of the side receiving the technology. Good managerial ability is an irrefutably large factor in good business results—it, too, has value. My major accomplishment was having convinced Philips of the value of this hidden asset, and they had accepted it. At the same time, that fee gave Matsushita Electric the heavy responsibility of guiding the new company in the right direction. Both Philips and we at Matsushita were aware of this condition, and Philips kept a close watch on our performance. As it turned out, the arrangement worked well, and ten years later, both companies had settled on a lower rate for technical expertise and management know-how.

The negotiations with Philips fully awakened me to the hidden value of managerial expertise. Matsushita Electronics Corporation did very well, and Philips was satisfied; our joint venture eventually surpassed the achievement of all its other affiliated companies.

15. Five-Day Workweek

Of all the elements in management, the central one is personnel. No operation works smoothly without good personnel administration. In fact, personnel may be the main factor behind the success or failure of a business.

It was in the interest of personnel that Matsushita Electric adopted the five-day workweek. It was already standard in American companies in 1960 but still unheard of in Japan. I made the decision in January that year to institute the five-day workweek five years from that time, in 1965, without reducing income levels.

Matsushita Electric was one of the first companies in Japan to institute the shorter workweek. My reasons for starting it at that time, when others had hardly considered it, concerned international competition. I believed Japan would face much greater competition in the future and that we should be prepared. In the early 1960s it became clear that Japan would have to liberalize trade in two or three years' time. When that happened, Japan had to be able to compete in the international market just to keep its head above water.

The electric appliance industry would be affected as much as other industries when liberalization brought in a host of foreign goods. If the imported products were better and cheaper, we would lose our customers. Our industry, like the others, faced ruin if we could not compete.

Matsushita Electric already had tough competition from other Japanese firms, but now we were faced with competition from many foreign companies. To meet it successfully meant that we had to fully automate Matsushita's production facilities, as well as raise the efficiency of its factories.

When I tried to pinpoint the key factor in becoming internationally competitive, I always came back to the same thing—labor efficiency. Our factory workers would have to be kept busier; our office personnel would have to cut their three-minute business calls to one minute. Both clerical and factory workers would have to be trained to work at a higher level of efficiency.

After an eight-hour day at an intensified tempo, the employees would be too exhausted to go on without a substantial break and still do good work. Eventually their health would suffer, too, without adequate rest to withstand the pace. That is why I decided they should be given two days off per week instead of the usual one. Two days would also give them more time for private pursuits and family life.

In 1960, American per capita productivity was more than twice that of Japan, and the American economy was still growing steadily. I knew that only when Matsushita Electric could perform at that level of productivity would we be able to compete effectively worldwide. At the January 1960 annual meeting to discuss management policy for the year ahead, I outlined my plans. "In five years' time we will be working five days a week," I said, "but our average wage levels should not be lower than those of our competitors. In fact, they should be higher."

We were flooded with criticism and charges of irresponsibility from the business and financial communities, the general public, even our own union. The members simply could not grasp how this seemingly costly and indulgent plan could possibly benefit the Japanese people. I persisted, however, and after four years, with only a year to go before the plan went into effect, the union began to understand the idea and agreed to work toward it. But it really took four years for our employees to get used to it and accept it.

Thus, we really had only one year for concrete preparations, and I was a little uneasy. Nonetheless, in April 1965, Matsushita Electric adopted the five-day workweek. It took time to get used to it, but I was satisfied, especially when I watched other companies follow suit later on.

16. The Fault May Be Yours

How quickly we note the failings of others instead of our own, and how easily we lay the blame for mistakes on someone else! We absolve ourselves all too casually, shrugging off our own responsibility. When a mistake is made, perhaps someone else is—or seems to be—responsible for it, but we cannot always be certain. We must not judge the cause by superficial results, for if we probe the situation, we may find that the mistake was partly our fault, too, and we must shoulder some of the blame. Whenever a mistake occurs, therefore, it is only fair to review all aspects of the situation, including indirect influences, before blaming someone else.

An incident that I shall never forget took place in 1964, during an important meeting that we called the Atami Conference. We had invited the presidents of one hundred-seventy sales and wholesale firms to Atami, a hot spring resort southwest of Tokyo, to familiarize ourselves with the management practices of the companies that handle our products.

There was a certain urgency in the meeting, because a severe recession that year had sapped the economy, and even some of the larger industrial and commercial concerns were in serious financial trouble. Bankruptcies were occurring with disturbing frequency. The electric appliance industry was pressed as hard as the others; some of its top-level companies were facing huge losses. The general situation demanded such a meeting, to exchange thoughts and seek the means to recoup.

Our guests spoke first. Many complained about large losses and blamed their financial plight on poor leadership by Matsushita Electric. "I inherited the business from my father," said one company president, "but recently I have been steadily in the red. What does Matsushita plan to do about this?"

Out of all the companies represented, only about twenty were making a small profit. All the rest were doing badly and they held us responsible, as they made very clear in the torrent of complaints they hurled at us.

The first day ended and the second day continued with speeches in the same vein—that Matsushita had not done very well by these companies that were so close to us. We made an attempt at analyzing their situations and parrying their accusations. "Your losses are your responsibility, not ours. What you really aim to get out of all this is some help from us, isn's it?" The discussion grew almost rancorous, as tempers on both sides flared and the arguments grew more heated.

As the second day drew to a close, it was disheartening to think that the meeting would end on such a divisive note. What in the world can we accomplish by a shouting match, I wondered. Our clients were insisting that Matsushita Electric shoulder all the blame, and we argued that their bad management was at fault. Neither side would budge an inch.

As I reflected more carefully on their grievances, and on our countercharges, it occurred to me that although their own management could have been responsible, perhaps that was only part of the problem. I began to see that their complaints about our shortcomings might be justified, and that perhaps carelessness in the planning and management of our business with client companies really had redounded on them heavily. If so, part of the blame, the greater part, rested with us, and the side that had to shape up was Matsushita Electric. We had been doing business with them for a long time and they had given us their trust. Perhaps we had been spoiled by their confidence in us, and were taking it too much for granted. Maybe our arrogance had been the root cause of this trouble.

I realized that, at this point, we of Matsushita Electric needed to remind ourselves of the company's original goal in business. In the early years, whenever we made a new product, we would take it to our wholesalers to get their reaction, and if they approved of the product, we sold it to them, pleased that they wanted to buy it. Later on, we began to lose sight of the idea of participation. Although I had sometims thought that our wholesalers lacked enthusiasm in selling certain products, that, too, was a mistake. When something did not sell, it was our fault, not our wholesalers'. The more I thought about it, the more convinced I was that Matsushita was largely responsible for many of its wholesalers' problems. When I addressed the meeting, I told them:

> Matsushita Electric is what it is today only because of your patronage and that of your parents and grandparents. My assertion that you are not managing your companies well was thoughtless, and a grave error on my part. You are bearing up under heavy losses now that were caused by our insufficient care and attention to your situation. As of today, Matsushita Electric will make some basic changes in its sales programs. We will see to it that your companies can operate with security, and we will make every effort to stabilize our industry.

Then I reminisced about our early attempts to sell lightbulbs. We had put a top price on those lightbulbs, urging our wholesalers to sell them at those prices in order to help our company grow. Happily for us, they cooperated, and we had been able to go on in the manufacture of other high quality products. Without the support and patronage of our sales and wholesale companies, I continued, we could never have moved so quickly and smoothly ahead.

As I spoke, remembering the enormous efforts we and all of them had invested together, I suddenly felt quite emotional, and I paused to wipe my eyes. Some in the audience were doing the same. One company president stood up and said, "The relationship between my company and Matsushita Electric is not simply financial. Its roots go far deeper. We have been harping about the responsibilities of Matsushita, but we have not been really fair. We are by no means blameless ourselves."

After two days of heated debate, the meeting came to a close on a heartwarming note. Both sides, remembering our long association, replaced their accusations with a renewed pledge to work together. We drew up a number of innovative sales plans, which were implemented with great enthusiasm. The result was gratifying: our sales companies, wholesalers, and retail outlets began to see their business grow better and better.

17. New Man at the Helm

MODERN people tend to be so caught up in the present that they do not see ahead with great clarity. Often we do not recognize the broad outlines of social currents, and we are apt to miss the larger movements in life. Yet to some extent, just to keep our society going, we have to be able to envision the future while we deal with the present.

In January 1977, Mr. Toshihiko Yamashita, then one of the youngest directors, took office as president of Matsushita Electric. This was an appointment that symbolized our vision of the twenty-first century. Over the years, my thoughts have shifted more and more to the future of Japan, as well as the world. I have tried to envisage, intuitively rather than analytically, the changes that will occur in our society, and I have tried to create an image of what life will be like in the next century.

In general, prosperity seems to shift from one area of the globe to another, following a natural flow of history. In the West, ancient Egypt and Greece were centers of prosperity, then Rome, Europe, and later North America. In the twenty-first century, I believe that the center of prosperity will be in East Asia, not the Middle East or Europe. If I am right, then Japan should be preparing for a new age of prosperity. One of our important tasks is to prepare our society for an era when prosperity is equally shared by all. The people of Japan have a challenge to meet, and I hope that Matsushita Electric will help them meet it with energy and optimism.

How should Matsushita Electric function and what should it do to help prepare the country for the new era? To us, this is a very serious question. To answer it, let us take a look at Matsushita Electric today. In 1978, it celebrated its sixtieth anniversary. In Japan, one's sixtieth birthday is called *honke-gaeri,* or returning to the start, meaning that one has come through a full sixty-year cycle according to ancient tradition, and has returned to the year of one's birth. In other words, in the year 1978, Matsushita Electric was symbolically reborn and its business life could start fresh.

If Matsushita Electric is to proceed firmly toward the next century, we must go back to our original purpose and seek a new direction that is geared to new times. We must renew our hearts and minds and open them to the ways we can help usher in the new prosperity.

While I was occupied with my thoughts, it happened that our chairman had to resign for reasons of health, and the president took over his position. The post of president was left vacant, to be filled by one of our four very competent vice-presidents.

But I sensed that we needed something different now. I wanted to see someone truly exceptional in that post, but what kind of person did Matsushita need to help lead Japan into the next century? How should we proceed to help prepare Japan for the new era of prosperity? First, I believed the next company president should be a man of innovation, able to translate his ideas into action, and young enough to keep working toward his goals for at least another decade. Both the outgoing chairman and president agreed.

Our criteria for selecting the president, which defied seniority, were considered somewhat unusual, and we knew they would raise eyebrows, but the old selection method was no longer adequate. We were on the threshold of a new, drastically changing era, in which Matsushita Electric should take a certain lead. It was appropriate, therefore, to follow an entirely new selection system that allowed consideration of a wider range of qualified people. We agreed that our new president could come from among the senior or even junior executives.

Thus, Mr. Yamashita's appointment in 1977 represented an entirely new leaf in the history of our company. And it carried with it our hopes and expectations that he will lead Matsushita Electric purposefully toward the next century, supporting the vital effort to prepare Japan for the new era.

18. Leaders of Tomorrow

WE talk about not seeing the forest for the trees, and indeed, we miss or ignore much that is right before us as we go through life, preoccupied with mundane daily problems. How much valuable time we waste on actions that have little purpose. There is much more to life than daily matters, however; we will still be around next month, next year, years to come.

What will life be like in the future? Will it be better, or worse, than today? No one can tell, but everyone hopes for a better future. Yet hope alone is impotent. We must act, but how?

In September 1978, the Matsushita School of Government and Management was created with the purpose of helping to train people capable of leadership in the twenty-first century. A press conference was held at the opening, and newspaper and magazine reports were both favorable and critical. The press had been unprepared for the relatively sudden appearance of the school.

I decided to open such a school out of concern about the future of Japan and the world, and my belief that we need to prepare competent people to help shape the future. I do not think we can be sanguine about our life today, and I started the school in the hope that it might prepare people with the ideas and ability to make our world better.

It has been nearly four decades since I founded PHP Institute to promote "peace and happiness through prosperity." At the time of its founding, immediately after World War II, Japan was a poor, stumbling country, and our government, which should have been taking the initiatives in shaping a better future for the nation, was too preoccupied with immediate demands. It was thwarting to know that so little was done, and so I decided to make an effort myself. I started PHP Institute because I was convinced that something *could* be done and that someone had to begin taking practical steps.

Japan recovered remarkably quickly after those desperate years, thanks to generous support coming from abroad, and to the diligence of the Japanese people. We have achieved material affluence, but in many ways our spiritual strengths have degenerated. Incidents of delinquency and suicides among the young are rising, and people seem to have forgotten how to behave in public. It seems quite acceptable today to immerse oneself totally in the pursuit of personal gain, and society suffers the disorder and violence of misplaced values.

There are several ways to look at these problems, but most people are concerned solely with the present: they have lost their vision of the future. If more could hold on to that vision and sincerely try to realize it, our society would regain its balance. Work would be more effective, as well as more productive, and our lives would be more worthwhile.

I believe in having a vision of the future, and in the importance of individuals and groups striving for a life of greater value. This does not mean binding ourselves to our jobs, or rigidly controlling our thinking and spontaneity. It means, rather, that each of us should draw upon his own merits and characteristics as fully as possible, freely and creatively. The future is ours. We must have the vision to build the most positive, supportive environment possible in the next century. We must start moving toward that future now.

The Matsushita School of Government and Management was born of my vision of a truly bright future for Japan. The outcome of my vision is not clear, but I believe we have a bright tomorrow as long as we have capable leaders.

Index

$78 40 net

308/85